Louisa May Alcott

ON RACE, SEX, AND SLAVERY

Louisa May Alcott

ON RACE, SEX, AND SLAVERY

Edited with an Introduction by Sarah Elbert

Northeastern University Press • Boston

Northeastern University Press

Frontispiece: Photograph of Louisa May Alcott taken at the time
of the Civil War. Courtesy of the Orchard House

Library of Congress Cataloging-in-Publication Data

Alcott, Louisa May, 1832–1888.
Louisa May Alcott on race, sex, and slavery / edited with an
introduction by Sarah Elbert.
p. cm.
Contents: M.L. — My contraband — Nelly's hospital — Colored
soldiers' letters — An hour — Elisha Harris, chapter X, The
freedmen of Mississippi.
ISBN 1-55553-308-6 (cloth : alk. paper). —
ISBN 1-55553-307-8 (pb : alk. paper)
1. United States—Social life and customs—19th century—Fiction.
2. United States—Race relations—Fiction.   3. Slavery—United
States—Fiction.   4. Afro-Americans—Fiction.   5. Sex role—Fiction.
I. Elbert, Sarah.   II. Title.
PS1016.E43   1997
813'.4—dc21   96-48085

Designed by David Ford

Composed in Stone Serif by Coghill Composition, Richmond,
Virginia. Printed and bound by Thomson-Shore, Inc., Dexter,
Michigan. The paper is Glatfelter Supple Opaque Recycled, an
acid-free stock.

MANUFACTURED IN THE UNITED STATES OF AMERICA
01 00 99 98 97   5 4 3 2 1

ACKNOWLEDGMENTS

*T*H E gathering of materials for this book depended on the kindness of many strangers who became friends, and the generosity of the "old" Alcott circle. Among these I would like to thank especially: Concord Free Public Library and Marcia Moss, Orchard House and Stephanie Upton, Madeleine B. Stern and Leona Rostenberg, Sidonie Smith, Patricia West, Carole Boyce-Davies, Elise Lemire, Mary Dougherty, the Victorian Studies Group, and U.S. Literature and History Seminar at S.U.N.Y. Binghamton, Nancy Henry, Bill Haver, Alice Rutkowski, Wendy Chimielewski, Tracey Jean Boisseau, Susan Belasco Smith, and the Alcott scholars who gathered in San Diego at the American Literature Association in 1996. Many critics improved the introductory essay, reading initial drafts and rereading later versions. George Cotkin, Carrie Kartman, Jennifer Langdon, Michael Pierson all made significant contributions to *Louisa May Alcott on Race, Sex, and Slavery,* even though their names do not appear on the volume. The same is true of John Weingartner, senior editor, and Ann Twombly, at Northeastern University Press, without whose enthusiastic support this book might never have come into being.

CONTENTS

INTRODUCTION

$\mathcal{O}$NE OF America's best-loved
stories opens on a snowy Christmas eve. No stockings are hung at the
fireplace for four young sisters, because their father is far away, "where
the fighting is," and their mother has proposed not having any presents
"because she thinks we ought not to spend money for pleasure, when our
men are suffering so in the army." Louisa May Alcott wrote and published
part I of *Little Women* in the winter of 1868 and part II in the spring of
1869; it was an instant best-seller, although the two volumes did not become one book until the 1880s. Concord, Massachusetts, the home of the
Alcott family, was not named as the scene for *Little Women,* just as the
Union Army and the Civil War fade into "the army" and "where the
fighting is." Alcott's partisanship comes through nevertheless; in the first
chapter Jo March unmasks her politics and her sexual frustration, remark-
ing that "keeping her temper at home was a much harder task than facing
a rebel or two down south." Literary historian John Limon asks, "What is
the Civil War doing in the first volume of Little Women?" He suggests
that the shadows of war provide more than autobiographical tribute, and
more than the occasion for a "female fantasy of liberated matriarchy."
The "Civil War is necessary so that Alcott can quarantine Jo from it."[1] In
other words, Jo's passion for Emersonian experience and self-reliance is
tamed into self-control and self-denial—but not quite. Louisa May Alcott
called herself a "fanatic" in the movement for abolition of slavery and
racial integration or, as it was called, "amalgamation of the races."[2] In the
last chapter of *Little Women* the surviving sisters are married and, with
their children, the family celebrates an apple harvest at Plumfield, the
boarding school run by Jo March and her husband, the "Professor." This
post–Civil War feminist dream reconstructs the nation as an extended
democratic family, and Alcott expands her sphere in *Little Men* (1871) and
Jo's Boys (1886). At the end of *Little Women,* the chorus of Plumfield, "a
happy, home-like place for boys who need teaching, care and kindness,"
performs a song written by Jo, with music by Laurie, and Mrs. March

shakes hands "with every one of the featherless birds, from tall Franz and Emil *to the little quadroon, who had the sweetest voice of all.*"[3]

Alcott's passionate concern for woman's rights and racial integration is tucked into a family reunion that surely represents national reunion. *Little Women*'s last chapter significantly evokes Louisa herself as Jo, her mother, Abigail May Alcott, as Mrs. March, and Bronson Alcott's unsuccessful interracial school as Plumfield, a mansion site inherited by Jo as a reward for domestic service to a rich aunt. Louisa May Alcott inherited the cause of woman's rights and abolition; she expanded them with self-conscious difference. In the fictionalized account of Louisa Alcott's civil war nursing service, *Hospital Sketches,* the abolitionist-feminist "Nurse Tribulation Periwinkle" hugged "Baby Africa," and as a war veteran, Louisa Alcott praised her friends' literacy classes for black soldiers and published the soldiers' letters. Cynthia Barton's recent biography of Abigail May Alcott notes that she was a pioneering social worker, and, with Louisa and Anna, she taught adult black women to read, write, and make out their bills for washing.[4]

Louisa May Alcott's boldest statements for human rights—her abolitionist interracial romances—preceded *Little Women* by more than five years. With "Colored Soldiers' Letters" and a "Sanitary Commission Report" of volunteers' reconstruction efforts during the Civil War, the romances are published together for the first time in this volume. "M.L." was written before the Civil War, in 1860, but the *Atlantic Monthly* declined to publish the story in that year because, Louisa wrote, "it is anti-slavery and the dear South must not be offended."[5] It was published as a serial in the *Commonwealth,* Boston's antislavery weekly newspaper in January and February 1863, when abolitionism and the Union cause were more popularly championed. The *Commonwealth,* edited by abolitionist friends of the Alcotts, also published her fictionalized memoirs of nursing service in their May and June issues of 1863; these were quickly picked up by James Redpath and reprinted as a successful book, *Hospital Sketches,* in that same year.[6] The book embodied the Union cause through the tender, "womanly" comradeship of wounded Union soldiers and the disciplined, maternal service of their nurses. The issue of racial amalgamation was lightly introduced as the "personal" politics of Nurse Tribulation Periwinkle, a "fanatic" in the cause. Alcott's openly abolitionist story, an interracial thriller, "The Brothers," was published in the *Atlantic Monthly* in November 1863; in subsequent publications it was retitled "My Contraband." Readers of the *Commonwealth* found "Colored Soldiers' Letters" in July 1864, and the slave rebellion story "An Hour" in November and December.[7]

Our understanding of these stories nearly one hundred and fifty years later is helped by placing the Alcotts' family drama within the history of woman's rights, white abolitionism, and public conflicts over "amalgamation," or "miscegenation," as it came to be called by the election year 1864. "M.L.," "The Brothers" ("My Contraband"), and "An Hour" deserve careful reading within Alcott's diverse body of works. As Elizabeth Young argues, "Women's Civil War fiction symbolically reimagines the relation between women and nationhood or, more specifically between the disorderly body of the woman author and the diseased body politic of the country at war. The nexus of disrupted and disruptive bodies emerges most clearly in the work of Louisa May Alcott. . . . Interpreted in the context of the Civil War, Alcott's work offers important insights into nine-

Nurse Tribulation Periwinkle holding Baby Africa. From Alcott's autobiographical *Hospital Sketches*. Courtesy of Concord Free Public Library.

teenth-century constructions of femininity, masculinity, authorship, war, and nationhood."[8]

The Alcotts' Armies of Reform

Bronson Alcott and Abigail May Alcott dedicated their marriage to spiritual perfectionism and social reform. They met in 1827 at the home of Abby's brother, the Reverend Samuel May. A young, Harvard-trained Unitarian minister, he zealously organized a common school reform convention in Connecticut that appealed to Bronson Alcott, a largely self-educated schoolmaster. Within a year Bronson had moved to Boston and, recommended by Abby and Sam May, he became headmaster of an experimental school; it was a privately endowed charity, his pupils drawn from Boston's immigrant population. Abigail May, admittedly in love with Bronson, hoped to teach with him, but her brother reminded her that personal involvement with Bronson precluded any "selfish" position for Abby May.[9] Later, in the famous Temple School, Alcott's assistants would include the Peabody sisters of Salem, Elizabeth and Sophia (Hawthorne), and the brilliant author and revolutionary Margaret Fuller. But Abigail May's recollection of the border between public and private conduct for ladies underscored a social problem evidenced even within the most radical reform ideology and culture before the Civil War. Was universal human potential sexually specific, and were men and women, by their very "natures," radically different emotionally and intellectually? Margaret Fuller, in *Woman in the Nineteenth Century,* named the problem that plagued Louisa May Alcott all her life and became an important theme in her works. Fuller wrote: "Ye cannot believe it, men; but the only reason why women ever assume what is more appropriate to you, is because you prevent them from finding out what is fit for themselves. Were they free, were they wise fully to develop the strength and beauty of women, they would never wish to be men."[10]

Expanding her society's publicly reiterated belief in the rights of man, Louisa May Alcott demanded both the abolition of slavery and political recognition of woman's rights. As a "sister woman," Louisa May Alcott championed the rights of slave women and mothers since, she argued, if there was one universal humanity and within it a common female experience, then, as her own mother had written in her journals, "the simple fact that the slavemother is not protected by law in her conjugal and material rights excites my imagination. . . . Every mother with a feeling heart and thinking head is answerable to her God, if she do not plead the cause of the oppressed."[11]

Similarly, the rights of man and woman, the Alcotts claimed, were safe only if *every* human being could earn a living and feed and protect a family. It was an article of faith among many conservative Northerners that the republic depended upon self-governing individuals raised in "little commonwealths." Voluntarism, the cornerstone of a virtuous republic, meant, for reformers, no forced unions of any kind, either domestic or civil; family discipline took the form of intimate scrutiny and the internalization of moral constraints. The sanctity of the individual was reiterated in their friend Ralph Waldo Emerson's famous series of essays titled "Experience," "Self-Reliance," "Friendship," and "Love."[12] The person who experienced life directly grew into spiritual and intellectual self-reliance, becoming an individual fully capable of republican self-government and unselfish friendship and love. Louisa May Alcott insisted that voluntary relationships could cross social boundaries of race as well as class and sex.

In 1829 a free black abolitionist, David Walker, published his "Appeal to the Coloured Citizens of the World," claiming that America "is as much our country as yours."[13] In the eighteenth and early nineteenth centuries many white antislavery advocates belived that slavery was contrary to republican principles, but they also believed that freed slaves and white persons of property and standing could not be citizens of the same republic. The American Colonization Society had been founded in 1816 and had sent its first black colonists to Africa four years later, where it subsequently founded Liberia. David Walker's "Appeal" spoke for the anticolonization black majority. The Alcotts joined a minority of white abolitionists now opposing colonization and calling for immediate emancipation. William Lloyd Garrison published the first edition of the *Liberator* in 1831, laying down a challenge: "I will not equivocate—I will not excuse—I will not retreat a single inch—AND I WILL BE HEARD."[14] That year also witnessed the Nat Turner Rebellion; slaveowners, although a minority of Southern whites, responded to the dual threat of slave rebellions and radical abolitionists (now almost solely Northerners) who were demanding immediate emancipation "without expatriation." Some people prayed for an imminent millennium, others feared anarchy, and the Alcotts worked for universal reform. In the midst of this ferment, on November 29, 1832, Louisa May, a second Alcott daughter, was born in Germantown, Pennsylvania.

Louisa's father and uncles, Samuel May and Samuel Sewall, were already members of the first Boston antislavery group; now they joined the American Anti-Slavery Society. Garrison would finally demand the admission of women into an integrated American Anti-Slavery Society in 1840, precipitating a further schism in the reform armies. Bronson Alcott had traveled as a young peddler in the South, walking back roads and selling Connecticut goods to slaveowners and free citizens alike. Having slept in slave quarters as the debt-ridden youngest son of a Spindle Hill farmer, he knew that he had neither property, education, nor family connections to separate him from slaves; only the color of his skin made him a free man. Sam May took only one young gentleman's tour into the South, after Harvard, and it was enough. He had passed a slave coffle by the roadside, "20 or 30 Negro men," irons about their wrists, with a heavy chain that was passed between them. Near "some young children lying upon straw, 4 or 5 black women were passing along the line and giving to each man a thick slice of coarse bread. . . . I am ashamed of my country and my race," he wrote.[15] In his first ministry he defended Prudence Crandall, a Quaker schoolteacher who accepted black pupils and was arrested by the local sheriff. May's house was an Underground Railway stop in Louisa's childhood, and his life was threatened when he became secretary of the Massachusetts Anti-Slavery Society. His sister Abby May Alcott also sheltered runaways and abolitionist agitators. She cheered her brother on in his effort, and for all her family pride in being related to Mrs. John Hancock, Abby May Alcott's sense of her own gentility did not blind her to the rights of "common" men and women.

Emancipation without emigration was hardly a popular cause among Northern white citizens, and anti-abolitionist mobs and riots occurred in major cities in the late 1830s and 1840s. In 1840, even the new Liberty Party, with James G. Birney as an antislavery candidate, did not campaign for immediate abolition but rather for "free soil," meaning a ban on slavery in the territories. Garrison called their demand "white-manism." In *Gentlemen of Property and Standing: Anti-Abolition Mobs in Jacksonian America,* historian Leonard Richards argues that anti-abolitionists repeatedly charged abolitionists with plans for "amalgamation," and that mob violence was most brutal in relation to any suggestions of interracial sex and marriage. Certainly urban newspapers in the 1830s insisted that amalgamation, real or imagined, provoked mob violence. Some historians, however, have argued that specific riots were motivated by economic fears. Richards disagrees, writing that "the behavior of the rioters indicates that the rhetoric of amalgamation reflected their deepest fears."[16]

Professor Elise Lemire cites a July 7, 1834, *New York Times* description of an integrated abolition meeting, held at a city church. The reporter insinuates that interracial sexual activities were taking place: "Clear, red and white were placed in unctuous communion with dingy black, and the rose of the West, and the coal-black rose of Congo, bloomed side by side, mingling their mutual sweets. There was no wasting of fragrance on the desert aire, for the delicate arome was inhaled by hundreds. The Reverend Doctor Cox presided, and opened the meeting with prayer."[17]

Lemire deepens Richards's analysis, offering substantial evidence from a variety of popular texts in the antebellum period that the "perceived connection between immediate abolitionism and amalgamation caused a crisis . . . within the discourses of middle-class romance which advocated pleasure and attraction in mate selection. What was the opposite of prejudice against blacks if it wasn't a complete embrace of them, even in the marital bed? Or, in the wake of emancipation, could all whites be trusted to have the sort of 'taste' which would ensure they would only be attracted to other whites? And what was 'taste' anyway?" In a fascinating discussion of novels and newspapers, Lemire excavates discourses that may well have inspired the gothic interracial stories written by Louisa May Alcott in the 1850s and 1860s; the constant discussion of interracial sex as either the major problem of slavery or the major problem of emancipation eroticized all aspects of white romantic culture.[18]

There is one cloudy but nevertheless intriguing racial enigma within the Alcott household itself involving Bronson Alcott, Abigail May, and Louisa. Although Abigail May was proud of the Sewalls, Quincys, and Hancocks in her lineage, her father, Colonel Joseph May, a Revolutionary veteran and a pillar of the First Unitarian Church, had a rather indistinct family tree. Family biographer Madelon Bedell notes that the Mays descended from an English shopmaster, John May, who arrived in America in 1640. His name was also spelled "Maies" or "Mayes," and he "was probably of Portuguese origin. The name is also Jewish; some of the original Maies may have been Portuguese Jews who fled the Inquisition."[19] Both Abigail May and Louisa May Alcott were dark complexioned (Louisa said "sallow" or sometimes "brown"), with dark hair and eyes; both had considerable tempers and admittedly passionate natures. Bronson himself was very blond and had blue eyes and, delightedly tracing his ancestry, persisted in believing that Anglo-Saxon "races" possessed more spiritually perfect natures, were generally "harmonious," and had more lofty intellects than darker-skinned people. He referred to Louisa and her mother at one difficult moment in Louisa's childhood as "two devils, as yet, I am not quite divine enough to vanquish the mother fiend and her daughter."[20] He joked that Louisa was a "true-blue May, or rather, a brown." He was hardly alone in believing not only that temperament is inherited but also that various religions, nations, tribes, and other groups were all distinct "races," characterized by specific temperaments, "gifts," and flaws that shaped their history. Louisa May Alcott's notions of race were shaped by daily family interactions as surely as they were by the larger cultural discourses. Louisa grew up calling herself "moody Minerva," and she compared herself unfavorably to her little sister May, a blue-eyed, wavy-haired blonde artist who combined work and pleasure in a more easy-going style.

Louisa Alcott's first published novel, the story of young girls's passage to womanhood through failed romance and marriage, was *Moods*. This novel is important to any analysis of Alcott's abolitonist, interracial stories because its secondary heroine, Faith Dane, is the principal heroine and narrative voice of Alcott's abolitionist thriller, "The Brothers," written in the same time period as *Moods*. Faith's independence and mature ability to create a refuge for Sylvia and other women similarly disadvantaged in *Moods* is explained by her direct experience with the worst tragedies of slavery and war, depicted in "The Brothers." The heroine of *Moods*, Sylvia Yule, is forced by social pressures as well as by her own loneliness to accept suitors before she has directly experienced life in the "real" world. Counseled by Faith Dane that she ought not to have married at all because she has an unstable, "moody" temperament, Sylvia is left at home to grow up, while her heroes go off together to fight for republican Italy. The Alcotts' friend and heroine, Margaret Fuller, an active correspondent in Europe during the revolutions of 1848, inspired *Moods'* fictional renditions of Italian republican struggles.[21] Abolition, racial amalgamation, and romantic nationalist revolutions were thus part of the Alcott family's social reality.

Margaret Fuller first entered Louisa's childhood as Bronson's assistant teacher in his Temple School. Although Fuller soon left to pursue her own work, she defended Bronson's character when the school failed because he held radical "Conversations" with pupils, probing the relationship between spiritual and physical (sexual) union and human births. By the time Louisa was five years old, the family had moved a number of times, from her birthplace to various neighborhoods in Boston. They ended up with a tiny home school on Beach Street, where the presence of their Negro schoolmate, Susan Robinson, raised fears of amalgamation even among the school's "liberal" parents. Soon Bronson and Abigail Alcott had no pupils besides their own children, and the Alcotts moved to Concord in 1840, where Bronson Alcott continued his "Conversations" with Ralph Waldo Emerson, Margaret Fuller, Henry David Thoreau, and the rest of the famous Concord circle. Bronson refused what he saw as meaningless work for meager wages, and, having no inherited wealth, the family—grown to four girls—endured years of freedom and poverty. The Alcotts' lives embodied the contradictions within American transcendentalism. As Bronson had said to his pupils, the reformers believed that every human being is God or has a God-like endowment of reason and imagination, and therefore all people are equal and gifted with divinely democratic potential. If every individual is a Supreme Being, however, then the individual is superior to the mass of humanity, and organized human groups are bound to confuse and corrupt individual integrity. Emerson held firm to individualism, but Henry David Thoreau, Margaret Fuller, the Reverend Theodore Parker, and the Alcotts were all drawn to the utopian socialist ideals growing in Europe and America. A wave of republican movements seemed to be sweeping the world in 1848, demanding the liberation of individuals from bondage. Once free to govern themselves, might the people not join in consociate families to produce and share the abundance they produced?

Meanwhile, in a rented Concord, Massachusetts, cottage, Abigail May Alcott, for the first time in her life doing her own housework and unsure of the means to pay for the family's wood, food, or rent, struggled with both poverty and pride. Feeling that she must sell her Hancock silver teapot to make ends meet, she nevertheless visited a "poor" family and kept her own family on two meals a day to bring a basket to that less fortunate household. With money from Emerson, Bronson Alcott temporarily escaped the domestic distress by traveling to England and visiting famous critics such as Thomas Carlyle and less well-known radicals, including utopian socialists who had named a hall in his honor. Joined by two of his English admirers, Charles Lane and Henry Wright, the reunited Alcott family then created their own spiritualist utopia on a small farm in Harvard, Massachusetts, naming the experiment "Fruitlands." A small band of reformers joined them in their cold-water utopia, sharing a limited vegetarian diet and uplifting philosophical conversations. From Abigail's point of view, the men talked, while the women worked; Louisa May Alcott, years later, poked fun at the hardships in a story, "Transcendental Wild Oats," which takes place at "Appleslump."[22] The adults, interested in the variety of American socialisms, visited other intentional communities where the problems of feeding families, nurturing spiritual needs, and providing a model for the rest of the world were being worked out.

Fruitlands, like Brook Farm, did not survive. Returning to Concord in 1845, the Alcotts found refuge in a house they called Hillside. One year later, Thoreau built his cabin at Walden Pond, where Bronson Alcott regularly visited his younger friend, calling him "the best republican in the Republic."[23] Louisa recalled botanical lessons with Thoreau, and her sister May later sketched his cabin and the pond. Thoreau's experience at Walden Pond became a hallmark of American environmentalism and individuality with his publication of *Walden* in 1854, but his naturalist's experiment was not a withdrawal from active resistance against tyranny. He opposed the expansionist war with Mexico (1846–1848) and slavery within the Union and the territories of the United States. In January of 1848, at the Concord Lyceum, he lectured about revolutions abroad: "All men recognize the right of revolution, that is, the right to refuse allegiance to and to resist the government, when its tyranny or its inefficiency are great and unendurable. . . . I think that it is not too soon for honest men to rebel and revolutionize."[24] *Walden* reflected Thoreau's concern about the survival capacity of a race he thought had grown soft and dependent upon manufactured goods and popular culture, a dependency he characterized, interestingly enough, by discussing, in *Walden*, the flimsy books in a series called "Little Reading." Tough-minded readers of past "heroic" generations, according to Thoreau, were being replaced by the mass readers of "little" books. Alcott's own *Little Women* was surely part of an even more solidly mass market system after the war. *Little Women* emphasized the girls' maturation through their own pilgrims' progress, and their burdens were most notably their unruly desires and their struggles for self-control. When Charles Brace came to Concord to lecture about the New York Children's Aid group on January 1, 1860, a small group of radical teachers, including Brace himself, Thoreau, and Alcott, discussed Darwin's newly available work, *The Origin of Species*. Replacing John Bunyan's emphasis on living for "the world to come," the new scientific paradigm, emphasizing evolutionary life on this earth, increasingly shaped both conservative and radical discourses of race, nation, and gender. Self-control, in uneasy tandem with self-reliance, became adaptive hallmarks of earthly progress.

The growing spirit of nationalism at home was tyranny to Thoreau and manifest destiny to President Polk and his supporters. Louisa May Alcott experienced her adolescence during a fever of expansionism: The Oregon Territory, Texas, California, Arizona, Nevada, Utah, Colorado, and Wyoming were becoming part of young America. Emerson's nationalist thoughts on democratic individualism were published and cherished by

French, Polish, and Italian radicals, though his own visit to Europe in the Year of Revolution only reinforced his suspicion of "the masses." Emerson agreed with the London *Times*'s condemnation of both Continental radicals and English Chartists' demands for political and social reform. Walt Whitman, nevertheless, hailed the Chartists, and his country woman Margaret Fuller, who was in Europe as correspondent for Horace Greeley's *New York Tribune,* condemned the London *Times* saying, "There exists not in Europe a paper more violently opposed to the cause of freedom than the Times."[25]

At Seneca Falls, New York, the first Woman's Rights Convention met in July 1848, basing its declaration firmly within the tradition of American nationalism. As historian Larry J. Reynolds points out, however, influential American newspapers described the Seneca Falls participants as revolution advocates, decrying that "it would go to our hearts to see them putting on the panoply of war, and mixing in scenes like those at which, it is said, the fair sex in Paris lately took prominent part."[26] The Alcotts were not present at Seneca Falls, but shortly thereafter Sam May attended the Syracuse, New York, Woman's Rights Convention, jubilantly reporting its proceedings to his sister and her family.

Margaret Fuller, having issued a clarion call to her sex in *Woman in the Nineteenth Century,* was in Italy, and her news of European revolutions was published in a series of twenty-four dispatches between 1847 and 1850 in the *New York Tribune.* Leaving the transcendental circle for New York in 1844, she had purposefully turned her efforts toward popular journalism in Greeley's paper. She moved abroad to active revolutionary experiences in Europe; as literary scholar Larry Reynolds describes, she traveled in Britain "in the open air on the top of a stagecoach, seeking out landscapes and people that Emerson ignored."[27] She toured mines, prisons, and Mazzini's school for poor boys. In France she observed child-care centers for working mothers, and everywhere she talked about Fourier and socialism with writers and revolutionaries, including George Sand and Adam Mickiewicz. In Italy she wrote to William Channing, who shared her letters with the Concord circle: "Art is not important to me now, I take interest in the state of the people, their manners, the state of the race in them. I see the future dawning; it is in important aspects Fourier's future."[28]

In Fuller's published works, "the race" was a universalist category, meaning the human race. Her private correspondence nevertheless reveals that she separated "the people" into culturally distinct groups; some were spiritually advanced, whereas others might be splendid physical specimens with primitive mental capacity. Fuller privately expressed fears for her own life and that of her lover as they were at the battlefront, in daily contact with the wounded and dying sons of Italy. The edited *Tribune* pieces of that period, however romantically abstract and addressed to a mass audience, were her most brilliant work, and friends eagerly awaited her promised "History of the Roman Republic." Neither the manuscript nor Fuller herself ever reached American shores; Margaret Fuller, her Italian husband, and their infant son died in a shipwreck just off Fire Island, New York. After the fall of republican Rome, and then Florence, Fuller had recognized that the struggle for democracy might last "fifty years, and the earth be watered with the blood and tears of more than one generation, but the result is sure, all Europe, including Great Britain . . . is to be under Republican Government in the next century."[29] Mazzini and Garibali were Fuller's friends and heroes, and ten years after her death, Garibaldi's letters in support of the emancipation of American slaves were printed in the *Commonwealth*, July 1, 1864, the same issue that carried Louisa May Alcott's "Colored Soldiers' Letters."

American historians frequently refer to the "crises of the 1850s," and it may well be argued that these were nationalist struggles; arguments over territory, slavery, and freedom boiled over into governance crises deep enough to become "an irrepressible conflict." The Compromise of 1850 was initially negotiated by Henry Clay and John C. Calhoun and then debated by a younger cadre of political leaders, including the antislavery William Seward, the cotton South's Jefferson Davis, and the increasingly important Illinois senator, Stephen A. Douglas. The truce finally made by these new leaders had one provision that angered the Alcotts and their friends more than any others; it called for a new and more effective fugitive slave law. Emersonian individualism had, to some extent, comforted Northern reformers with the belief that each state's laws governed its own consciences. Under the Fugitive Slave Law, however, blacks accused of escaping from slavery had no rights to jury trials; indeed, they could not testify in their own behalf. A slaveowner's affidavit of ownership was sufficient for a federal judge or commissioner to return either fugitives or alleged former slaves to the South. Personal liberty laws passed in some Northern states offered only illusory protection to black citizens. By some accounts, at least six hundred runaway slaves lived in Boston in fear of the new Fugitive Slave Law. Emerson, roused by the challenge to his own freedom of conscience, declared it "a filthy enactment" and one that he would not obey.[30]

The Boston Committee of Vigilance, organized to protect runaway slaves, was headed by the Reverend Theodore Parker (portrayed by Louisa

Alcott as the Reverend Power in her novel *Work: A Story of Experience* [1873]).[31] Bronson Alcott was a charter member of the group, which succeeded in rescuing a slave called Shadrach from the federal courthouse but failed to rescue another black, Thomas Simms, from prison. In 1854, President Pierce sent a U.S. marshal to seize a runaway slave, Anthony Burns, from Boston. The resistors included Thomas Wentworth Higginson, who later commanded a black regiment, and Bronson Alcott. They organized a rescue from the courthouse under cover of a mass meeting to be held in Faneuil Hall. On the evening of May 27, Higginson ran up the steps of the courthouse and confronted a sheriff, who slammed the door in his face. A black abolitionist, never named, hammered another door open with a heavy beam, and as the door opened, Higginson and his comrade ran in and were assaulted by police with clubs. A shot killed the sheriff, and Higginson was badly beaten and thrown outside. Bloodied but unyielding, he yelled for support. Only two men came forward—Seth Webb, Higginson's Harvard classmate, and the grey-haired and unarmed Bronson Alcott. According to Higginson's memoir of the event, Alcott asked, "Why are we not within?" Higginson replied, "Because these people will not stand by us." Alcott stood silently for a long moment and then walked slowly down the courthouse steps. To Higginson, who had previously thought Alcott more than a little fuzzy minded and egotistical, the older man behaved "as well as Plato or Pythagoras might have done," and "all minor criticisms of our minor sage appear a little trivial when one thinks of him as he appeared that night."[32]

It took two thousand federal troops with drawn bayonets to return Anthony Burns to Virginia slavery. A Northern abolitionist purchased Burns's freedom a few months later, and the latter received a scholarship to Oberlin College School of Divinity. Certainly the incident united Massachusetts in favor of personal liberty, although not for immediate emancipation. Lawful enslavement of people by virtue of their skin color deeply affected Louisa May Alcott, and the fragility of independence was to haunt her life and fiction. If middle-class security was based on skin color and upon differences supposedly inherent even between "white" men and "white" women, Alcott chose to be identified as a working woman all her life.

Living in Boston, with Bronson still earning a pittance with his "Conversations" and with her mother and sisters working in and out of the house, Louisa May Alcott worked as maid, a seamstress, a teacher, and a governess. Though she thought of becoming an actress, "with plenty of money and a very gay life," she scribbled at "romantic" stories, not sure whether her needle or her pen would provide independence. During her own years of crisis, Alcott strategically published some stories anonymously and some domestic tales and poems under her own name, whereas her thrillers appeared in popular sensation papers. In *Little Women*, part I, Jo March secretly writes her stories in the attic, and "The Rival Painters" appears in the fictitious newspaper *Spread Eagle*. In reality, Alcott's "The Rival Painters: A Tale of Rome" appeared in 1852 in the *Olive Branch*.[33] Literary traditions as well as the experiences of Alcott's cosmopolitan circle of reformers certainly predisposed her to set romantic thrillers in Europe and the Caribbean, while her personal and familial need to publish her writings for a living meant that she wrote sensationalist thrillers, domestic stories, children's stories, and importantly, abolitionist adventure stories at top speed and almost simultaneously. Characters jumped from the pages of one story to another, as did her mixed settings; she deployed mulattos, mulattas, white women, white men, as well as African-born heroes and heroines in relationships that often radically transgressed conventional genre boundaries. Perhaps the writer herself was beginning to experience a sense of power that she inscribed to her characters. As Madeleine Stern, Alcott's modern biographer, points out, in the chapter in part II of *Little Women* called "Literary Lessons," Jo March "began to feel herself a power in the house, for the magic of the pen, her 'rubbish' turned into comforts for them all." In that chapter, Alcott revealed the existence of several of her anonymous and pseudonymous thrillers, many of them finally traced and republished over a hundred years later by Leona Rostenberg and Madeleine B. Stern.[34]

As Louisa May Alcott struggled for self-reliance, the Supreme Court of the United States, Justice Roger Taney presiding, decided that slaves were property, that no person of African descent qualified as a citizen, and that therefore Dred Scott, a Missouri slave taken to Illinois (a free state) and then to Wisconsin territory could not sue for his freedom. President Buchanan supported the Dred Scott decision, and, in 1857, he also supported the admission to the Union of Kansas as a slave state. The controversy turned the territory into Bloody Kansas, and John Brown became an armed revolutionary leader. Kansas entered the Union finally as a free state, but the crisis catapulted one senate election into national importance, pitting Stephen A. Douglas against Abraham Lincoln, candidate of the new antislavery Republican Party. Exciting fragments of their debates reached Massachusetts papers, but the full speeches of each man were printed separately in the pro-Douglas *Chicago Times* and the pro-Lincoln *Chicago Press* and *Tribune*.[35] The debates were published in their entirety only in the spring of 1860, in time for the presidential campaign, when they became a best-seller. By the time he was nominated at the Illinois Republican Convention, Lincoln was insisting that slavery must not be allowed to spread into the territories and that it was to be accepted only as a temporary condition. There he argued, "A house divided against itself cannot stand. I believe this government cannot endure, permanently half *slave* and half *free*." Lincoln had already contended that

> there is a natural disgust in the minds of nearly all white people to the idea of an indiscriminate amalgamation of the white and brown races. . . . Judge Douglas . . . finds the Republicans insisting that the Declaration of Independence includes ALL men, black as well as white; and forthwith he boldly denies that it includes negroes at all, and proceeds to argue gravely that all who contend it does, do so only because they want to vote, eat, and sleep, and marry with negroes! He will have it that they cannot be consistent else. Now I protest against that counterfeit logic which concludes that, because I do not want a black woman for a *slave* I must necessarily want her for a *wife*. I need not have her for either, I can just leave her alone. In some respects she certainly is not my equal; but in her natural right to eat the bread she earns with her own hands without asking leave of any one else, she is my equal and the equal of all others.[36]

Elise Lemire points out that both Lincoln and Douglas used amalgamation as a threat. Douglas saw opposition to the Dred Scott decision as resulting in "indiscriminate amalgamation," and Lincoln saw the spread of slavery resulting in the already well-known sin of amalgamation. Their argument mirrored the paradox of abolitionism and anti-abolitionism. Antislavery advocates had long argued that the inherent sin of the institution lay in its powers of coercion, powers that corrupted the slaveowner perhaps more than the enslaved. Harriet Beecher Stowe made that argument repeatedly in *Uncle Tom's Cabin*. Written as a direct attack on the Fugitive Slave Law, the novel developed "Uncle Tom" as a hero whose black body was brutally tortured and murdered, though his white soul was free. The mulatto and quadroon bodies in Stowe's fiction were consistent with most white antislavery arguments—the "tragic" results of degraded slaveowners' passions. Their excess passions were doubly "unnatural" since "natural disgust," as Lincoln termed it, accompanied any idea of sexual union between black and white. (The slippage between rape and mutual consent was evident in Northern and Southern states' laws against interracial marriages.) Before and during the Civil War, antislavery writers repeatedly stressed the horror of meeting slaves or freedmen and -women whose skin color was as white or whiter than the writers' own complexions. Selling the masters' mixed-race children away was described as both unnatural and dangerous because their descendants could turn up anywhere as "white"; and, being "white," they quite possibly had inherited the "Anglo-Saxon" passion for freedom and a "natural" instinct for violent resistance to slavery. Indeed, Stowe's mulatto and quadroon characters themselves "pass" as white during their escape to freedom and reunited family life. Stowe, however, sent her mixed-race families back to Africa, warning readers of the "San Domingo" possibilities inherent in emancipation without repatriation. In Louisa May Alcott's youth, both proslavery and antislavery romances often titillated white readers by revealing the "one drop" of hidden African blood that doomed the couple. The invisibility of racial difference, however, clearly revealed the social construction of race itself.[37]

Alcott recorded her admiration for Stowe's novel in her journals. Alcott's own abolitionist fiction would, nevertheless, favor interracial marriage and armed slave rebellion if "voluntary" emancipation was not speedily granted by slaveowners. "M.L.," written in the wake of Harpers Ferry, offers redemption to one quadroom former slave through a white woman's self-sacrificing love. As a Christian offering to the abolitionist cause, "M.L.," as we shall see, slips across the literary border from gothic to what Susan Gillman calls "race melodrama."[38] In "The Brothers" ("My Contraband"), written after the Emancipation Proclamation, her contraband hero "had no religion, for he was no saintly 'Uncle Tom' and Slavery's black shadow seemed to darken all the world to him, and shut out God." The tale, once again, is a melodramatic response to a historical dilemma; redemption is finally linked to a heroic death in military action at Fort Wagner.

One famous incident particularly confirmed Louisa's desire to enter the fight for emancipation as a "soldier" herself and to write graphically about men and women, enslaved and freeborn, who fought and fell in love across social boundaries. By 1857 the Alcotts, following the death of Louisa's youngest sister, Beth, finally moved into their own Orchard House in Concord. In 1859, Captain John Brown spoke in Concord at a New England Emigrant Aid Society meeting organized by the Alcotts' close friend, Franklin Sanborn, an abolitionist. The Alcotts, Sanborn, and Thoreau were part of the conspiracy to raise money for John Brown's raid—with a small force of black and white volunteers—against the federal arsenal at Harpers Ferry, Virginia, in hopes of seizing guns and arming a slave rebellion. Brown and his eighteen raiders attacked and seized the arsenal, but the slave uprising was prevented; local citizens, militia men, and then United States troops commanded by Robert E. Lee took the arsenal, killing ten of the raiders. Brown surrendered and was tried in Virginia for treason against the state. Found guilty, he was hanged on December 2, 1859, and the remaining six members of his raid were also tried and hanged.

Brown's trial spurred the Alcotts and Sanborn to plan an assault upon the jail to free him. Finally they asked Thomas Wentworth Higginson to lead a rescue party, and when that plan faded, every member of the Concord and Boston circle of reformers tried to stay the execution or, at least, bring comfort and medical supplies to the jail. Elizabeth Peabody traveled to Virginia to beg the governor for clemency. It was no use, and Concord went into mourning on the day of the hanging, with a public memorial service organized by Thoreau. Alcott wrote a poem, "With a Rose That Bloomed on the Day of John Brown's Martyrdom," observing that "No

Louisa (seated), Bronson, and Abigail May Alcott, Anna Alcott Pratt, and children in front of Orchard House, Concord, Massachusetts. Courtesy of Orchard House.

monument of quarried stone, no eloquence of speech,/Can grave the lessons on the land his martyrdom will teach." Sanborn arranged to have the poem published in the *Liberator*.[39] After receiving a federal subpoena to testify about his part in the Harpers Ferry raid, Sanborn was handcuffed and arrested in the middle of the night; he was eventually cleared, but Concord supporters, including Louisa May Alcott herself, formed a vigilante committee to protect him and presented him with a revolver. Sanborn and the Alcotts' friend Moncure Conway were instrumental in gathering the younger reform generation together to perform radical actions. They also actively helped Louisa May Alcott write for the cause and publish in the intersecting networks of commercial and abolitionist press. In July 1860, Mrs. John Brown (called Mrs. Captain) was a guest at Orchard House, where the Alcotts invited supporters to meet her. Louisa May Alcott described her as "a tall stout woman, plain, but with a good strong face, and a natural dignity that showed she was something better than a 'lady' though she did drink out of her saucer and used the plainest speech."[40] Alcott's poem about John Brown was reprinted in Redpath's *Echoes of Harper's Ferry*. In this same period, Louisa heard Harriet Tubman describe her rescue trips to and from the South, and Tubman would appear in Alcott's novel *Work* as Hepsey, a former slave, working and saving her wages to free her family.[41]

The Fugitive Slave Act, Harpers Ferry, and most directly resistance to slavery within her own family's circle of friends confirmed Alcott as a writer whose art was consciously in the service of her political commitments. Writing and publishing were increasingly means to self-reliance, a full personhood, and to a social authority usually denied to women. Authors were authorities; readers properly read to learn the right way to live. The problem, of course, was negotiating cultural boundaries to publish in the expanding mass market for popular literature. The possibility of earning a living as a writer gradually became a reality; women could write, especially for other women readers, and popular newspapers and periodicals took advantage of cheap female authors, allowing them to publish discreetly under pseudonyms. Equally important, there was no professional training required; no traditional gatekeepers barred her way. The Alcotts were poor but genteel, and as activists in a reform era, they also had influential friends among literary patrons and publishers. By the mid-1860s, Louisa's journal entries refer increasingly to business with publishers and editors, as often as they mention her efforts at sewing, teaching, and housekeeping for a living.

The Concord reform circle gathered formally when Alcott lost another friend and mentor, Henry David Thoreau, who died at the age of forty-four of advanced tuberculosis on May 6, 1861. He had organized the tributes to John Brown; now the Alcotts and Emerson arranged the services for Thoreau. He was buried in Sleepy Hollow Cemetery, near the Alcotts' plot, and Louisa fictionalized him as a seductive though overpowering revolutionary hero, Adam Warwick, in *Moods,* the novel she began in 1860 and worked on intermittently for the next four years.[42]

America's Civil War finally burst out, its first skirmishes reported in the newspapers before Lincoln was inaugurated in 1861. The South seceded, and the Southern Confederacy marshaled eight thousand men at Harpers Ferry, resolved to capture Washington and chase "the Illinois Ape" back to Illinios. Lincoln's Republican supporters became "Black Republicans," and Alcott numbered herself among them.

Portrait of John Brown hanging in the Alcotts' living room at Orchard House. The Alcotts were active supporters of John Brown and sheltered his wife and daughters after his death. Courtesy of Orchard House.

Louisa was thirty years old and determined to go to war, and finally she did, in December 1862, arriving for duty at the Union Hotel Hospital in the Georgetown area of Washington. Just two years earlier Louisa had written to young Alf Whitman, one of Frank Sanborn's pupils:

> There was always something very brave and beautiful to me in the sight of a boy when he first "wakes up" and seeing the worth of life takes it up with a stout heart and resolves to carry it nobly to the end through all disappointments and seeming defeats. I was born with a boys nature and always had more sympathy and interest in them than in girls, and have fought my fight for nearly fifteen (years) with a boys spirit under my "bib and tucker" and a boys wrath when I got "floored", so I'm not preaching like a prim spinster but freeing my mind like one of "our fellows", and as such I wish you all success, a cheerful heart, an honest tongue and a patient temper to help you through the world for its roughgoing and up hill work much of the way.[43]

Dorothy Dix and Clara Barton usually recruited married women for nursing service because young, romantic spinsters might "give way under the labors which required a mature strength, a firm skill in all household duties." Alcott's friends and family connections were as influential politically as they were in writing and publishing, and they helped her join the nursing service. The Mays, Sewalls, and Alcotts had worked for the war effort, organizing fairs and benefits and auctioning off everything from quilts to pies and poetry; Louisa herself was one of three hundred women sewing Union uniforms in the Concord Town Hall.[44] They also staffed the local, regional, and national offices of the Sanitary Commission, which organized Union medical aid to troops and relief for veterans and their families. When Alcott finally received her orders to report to the hospital, she was still poor but not entirely unknown as a professional writer and a level-headed war worker. Alcott set off with a small trunk packed by her mother and sisters, with the aid of Sophia Hawthorne, and a small supply of cash to supplement army pay and army-style rations. Feeling like the "son of the household," she was off to war, her meals and twelve dollars a month promised by the government.[45] Washington was not thought of as a safe post, and Union troops were garrisoned everywhere. The makeshift hospital was half boarded up against artillery fire, and the wards were fashioned from old hotel ballrooms, suites, and reception areas. Alcott kept her journals and wrote letters home describing her tiny bedroom, shared with two other nurses and furnished with one closet, their trunks, one chair, and a tin saucepan that doubled as their mirror.

On the first morning Louisa witnessed a death on her ward, nursed both

Introduction

artillery wounded and pneumonia cases, and cared for a man dying from a fatal shot through the lungs. On a typical day she would jump "up at six, dress by gaslight, run through my ward, and throw up the windows, though the men grumble and shiver; but the air is bad enough to breed a pestilence." Accustomed to home nursing and even to heavy work outdoors, Alcott still found this regime grueling and hard to bear; amputations, she said, were the worst part—she had to assist in the painful process of picking out bone fragments from shattered limbs, always wishing, she wrote, "that the doctors would be more gentle with my big babies."[46]

In public and private writings she described herself as a mother to these men, some merely boys, ill and dying far from home. She scrounged up bandages and linen, washed all the patients, and wrote letters home to the soldiers' families as well as to her own asking for fruit, jams, pickles, and anything else that might supplement the salted, fried beef, frequently moldy bread, and the watery coffee. The nurses had no rest all day, working through supper at five o'clock and the doctors' last rounds, following

"Leaving the Hospital Tents for the Battle Field." Engraving by G. E. Perine and Co., New York. The Concord Volunteers served at Gettysburg, where Sanitary Commission field hospitals and soup kitchens served the wounded. From Frank Moore, *Women of the War: Their Heroism and Self-Sacrifice* (Hartford, Conn., 1866).

up with the administration of medicine and sleeping potions. Then, as Alcott wrote, "night nurses go on duty, and sleep and death have the house to themselves."[47] She took night duty herself in order to tour Washington several times during the day; she sat in Senator Sumner's chair in the Senate chamber, imagining herself thrashing his assailant, Senator Preston Brooks.

She found, not surprisingly, that her sister nurses were not often amalgamationists. Angered by those who "were willing to be served by the colored people, but seldom thanked them, never praised and scarcely recognized them on the streets," she fashioned one incident into a scene for *Hospital Sketches*.[48] As Nurse Tribulation Periwinkle cuddled a contraband baby in her arms while stirring a pot of gruel, a Virginia nurse sniffed, "Gracious how can you? I've been here six months and never so much as touched the little toad with a poker." Nurse Periwinkle's response was to "kiss the toad."[49] These journal entries and letters, edited into *Hospital Sketches,* brought Alcott serious literary notice and five cents a copy for the first Redpath edition of one thousand. *Sketches* was a substantial contribution to the Union cause and to abolition, but Nurse Tribulation Periwinkle is, at first, a comical, Dickensian narrator. Gradually she finds a more substantial voice, firmly declaring herself a "woman's rights woman." She finally emerges as a hospital angel, gathering the dying John Sulie, a handsome soldier, into her arms, but only as his absent mother might do: "straightaway my fear vanished, my heart opened wide and took him in, as gathering the bent head in my arms, as freely as if he had been a little child, I said, 'Let me help you bear it John.' "[50]

Alcott's hospital experience was brief—she contracted typhoid pneumonia, and, neglecting to nurse herself, she was in a dangerous state by the time Bronson Alcott was summoned to Washington on January 21, 1863, to take her, only semiconscious, home to be nursed by her mother and sister. She had, however, been in Washington on New Year's Day when Lincoln's Emancipation Proclamation took effect, declaring slaves in the rebellious states "thenceforth and forever free." Importantly, the proclamation also stated that the government would no longer "repress such persons in any efforts they may make for their actual freedom." Alcott "threw open her windows and cheered in answer to the shout of colored men in the street below. All night they tooted and ramped, fired crackers, and sang Glory hallelujah."[51] Just a few days before, she had helped receive some of the 9,600 casualties of Fredericksburg, where General Burnside had mounted an unsuccessful attack against the entrenched forces of Stonewall Jackson and Robert E. Lee.

There were two more long war years, but Louisa May Alcott was permanently invalided home. The heroic doses of calomel prescribed for her fever slowly ate away her nervous system, causing lifelong debilitation; she thereafter had painful joints, swollen limbs, and headaches that could not be soothed by sleeping powders, hypnosis, or opium derivatives.[52] What transpired in her feverish state and in the long recovery that followed apparently became part of the gothic thrillers that were linked powerfully to her abolitionist stories. She wrote both kinds of tales in the aftermath of her illness. In her delirium, she dreamed that she had married "a stout, Handsome Spaniard, dressed in black velvet, with very soft hands, and a voice that was continually saying, 'Lie Still, my dear!' " Awake, she identified the voice as her mother's. Abigail May Alcott was stout, "Spanish" looking, and usually a gentle comfort to her daughters; but Louisa's "Spanish spouse" was not a comfort, and she explained that, mixed with her mother's presence, was an "awful fear" of this husband who "was always coming after me, appearing out of closets, in at windows, or threatening me dreadfully all night long." She appealed to the pope, her family said, in "something meant for Latin," and then felt she had gone to heaven and didn't like it, "with people darting through the air in a queer way, all very busy, and dismal, and ordinary. Miss Dix, W. H. Channing, and other people were there; but I thought it dark and 'slow' and wished I hadn't come." The fantasies finally included a Baltimore mob, and Louisa being hung for a witch, burned, stoned, and otherwise maltreated. She was also "being tempted to join Dr. W. and two of the nurses in worshipping the Devil. Also tending millions of rich men who never died or got well."[53]

Louisa May Alcott was certainly near death, and despite her liberal commitment to "the church of one," she may have feared for her soul as well as for her body. She had also experienced what Dix and Barton had feared with single nurses—she had been in close contact with strange, and often heroic, men. She had washed, nursed, fed, and comforted men who returned her devotion with small gifts, thanks, and affection, and some of them continued to write to Miss Alcott for years afterward. She said nothing specific in her letters about race, mentioned no contraband men; but the wards were staffed with contraband orderlies, and the streets were filled with colored and white men, and war nurses, and visitors, all mixing "promiscuously on the streets." She was herself a dark-skinned "white" woman with a "boy's nature" and a writer's gift. Whatever she felt in the confusion of gender and race was released in her delirium, and it found outlet in her fictions.

Less than a year after the Emancipation Proclamation, in December of 1863, a new word appeared, "miscegenation." An anonymous New York pamphlet, purporting to be pro-abolition and amalgamationist, was published under the title *Miscegenation: The Theory of the Blending of the Races, Applied to the American White Man and Negro.*[54] It was actually written by David Goodman Croly and George Wakeman, editor and writer of the Democratic *New York World* newspaper. It presented the Republican Party as favoring the transfer of Southern plantations to black troops, and it claimed that, "When the President proclaimed Emancipation he proclaimed also the mingling of the races. The one follows the other as surely as noonday follows the sunrise." The pamphlet explained that the new word "miscegenation" was a combination of the Latin word "miscere," to mix, and "genus," meaning race. Croly and Wakeman claimed that amalgamation was a poor term, properly referring to the union of metals with quicksilver. The pamphlet caught on—by early 1864 even Horace Greeley approvingly accepted the new word in the abolitionist *New York Tribune.* Sidney Kaplan analyzed the journalists' fraud in the 1940s in *The Journal of Negro History,* providentially written during the same period that Leona Rostenberg first identified the hidden thrillers of Louisa May Alcott, written in the 1860s, and Margaret Fuller's Roman letters.[55] The current historical analyses by David Roediger and Eric Lott of interracial conflict as an inevitable component of modernity refocus our understanding of Croly and Wakeman's invention of a new scientific term derived from scholarly Latin, "miscegenation" replacing the earlier "amalgamation"—a blacksmith's process. The authority of Darwinian scientific discourse was deployed by the rapid firepower of mass media. Within a few months, other American papers were using the term "miscegenation," and even after the fraud was revealed, the London papers recognized that "Speakers and writers of English will gladly accept the word 'miscegenation' in place of the word amalgamation."[56] As Elise Lemire points out, scholars "must read the pamphlet with an ear for (this) doubleness," meaning that the writers cited all the "physical, intellectual, and moral traits which were thought to be race traits." By citing all the imagined and real sources—scientific, religious, and political—that seemed to be arguing for "natural" mixing, the pamphlet prompted abolitionists publicly to approve arguments attributed to them there. Publicly admitting what many radical abolitionists had earlier kept delicately quiet gave even more fuel to anti-abolitionists claims about emancipation. Lemire goes on to list the pamphlet's main themes: that equality of classes results in interracial sex, that there is a scientific basis for the naturalness and benefits of racial mixing, and that "opposites attract."

Emancipation created a class of free black workers, and mixing the races in the labor market led to social and sexual mixing, thereby removing the one preferential card held by the "white" working class. Indeed, the middle class, a subsequent pamphlet argued, had as much or more to fear because a white woman interested in upward social mobility might well prefer a wealthy black man or an elected black governor as a husband.[57] The *Commonwealth,* in the issues featuring Louisa May Alcott's "M.L.," under "Miscellaneous" reported on a planter's widow in Arkansas who, finding herself with land, thirty Negroes, and a debt of ten thousand dollars, was prepared to sell the slaves and a portion of the land. The paper reported, however, that the foreman on the estate, "himself a negro and a slave," talked to the other slaves and proposed that they farm the plantation and work off the debt. The Connecticut-born widow agreed to his proposal, the slaves raised a fine crop of cotton, and they paid off the debt in two years without "a white man on the premises." They proceeded to work the plantation up to a value of $100,000 over a period of ten years. When the war made communication with the plantation impossible, the lady remained there with the Negroes and her eldest son who, the correspondents feared, might have been "forced" into the Rebel army.[58] Left unanswered but surely a titillating question in readers' minds was, What happened to the lady and her "humane and heroic negro" foreman? As Lemire argues, economic equality and class parity could lead readers to think in very conflicted, but aroused, ways about interracial sex.

In Garibaldi's letters, forwarded to the *Commonwealth* by a Manchester member of the Union and Emancipation Society, the Italian leader called himself "a son of the people," nourishing "a great affection for the laboring classes who throng your noble country." His words deserve reading once again because they exemplify the links between emancipation, brotherhood, and "the laboring class" rising in solidarity, a spectre more to be feared than exalted, as some saw it. Garibaldi wrote:

> Union! Is it not by union that nations should be bound together and become as brothers? Has not the human family, for many centuries, while marching onward on the glorious career of progress, exemplified by our Saviour, wished for the same union, though often retarded by corruption and tyranny? Emancipation! May God bless you! What mission is more glorious than that of emancipating the slaves?[59]

Senator Sumner, in that same issue, editorialized that the freedmen desired work and that the intervention of the national government was necessary, citing the Emancipation Proclamation's words to freedmen— "that in all cases when allowed they labor faithfully for reasonable wages."[60] Anti-abolitionists used those words to frighten white workers with competition from freed slaves, who were expected to pour into the industrial labor force. The Freedmen's Bureau was challenged in Congress and debated in newspapers on grounds of its "miscegenation" process and its deadly effect on white citizens. The new propaganda about miscegenation, linking sex, race, and class in powerful "evolutionary" discourses, suggested a threat to the survival of the white race, indeed, even the death of the white race, as it inadvertently revealed the social, rather than biological, construction of race.

Bodies of Fiction

Lora Romero brilliantly argues, following Foucault, for a kind of "simultaneity and co-implication" of heroism and sentiment in nineteenth-century fictions.[61] Adventure fictions, she argues, "because they so often unfold on borders between 'civilized' and 'savage' frequently engage questions about the survival of the races."[62] She is discussing specifically James Fenimore Cooper's *The Last of the Mohicans*, the antebellum "Cult of the Vanishing American," and Thoreau's *Walden*. Recalling Foucault's argument that "power legitimates and incarnates itself through the right of the social body to ensure, maintain, or develop its life," Romero reiterates, "racial holocaust becomes 'vital' to its expression." She also persuasively argues that the much-discussed feminization of American society "itself participates in the imperialist nostalgia of the discourse it analyzes."[63] In the "feminization" interpretation, maternal influences clearly presented as civilizing forces in sentimental antislavery fiction, such as Alcott's *Hospital Sketches* of the Union's female nursing service, extend domestic surveillance and, by promoting the public role of women in bureaucratic social service after the war, invade the presumably sacred and resistant stronghold of private, working-class family life. The revisionist narrative of modernization, although compelling in many ways, also romanticizes a mythic time when "authority represented simple physical superiority . . . Foucault's temporalization of the difference between discipline and punishment."[64] In other words, "feminization" of society meant the substitution of "loving," intimate surveillance for earlier "patriarchal" domination enforced by physical punishment and public torture and execution.

Revising the revisionists' insights about the body politic stimulates our appreciation of the double bind in Alcott's life and fiction between 1860 and 1865. Specifically, paying attention to the violence Alcott wrote into public and private texts connects her own bodily torment with the body of her works. A Spanish spouse (and "Spanish" was frequently a code word for black) was the projection of the overworked and disciplined "son of the household," when, like her soldier patients, she was rendered helpless by typhoid fever. Louisa dreamed that she had married, and marriage invoked the injunction that women "suffer and be still." Although Abby Alcott was a beloved "Marmee" to her girls, she was also a passionate woman, married for love to a man who, more than once, retreated into chastity and male companionship, most famously including his close friendships with Charles Lane, Emerson, and Thoreau. His "divinity" was, he felt, compromised by the demands of supporting children and household through an ordinary workingman's wages. He wrote admiringly of the daring Margaret Fuller, enjoyed his relationships with young teaching assistants, and, as an older "sage," had the pleasure of conversations and walks with doting younger women of the circle. The Alcotts' marital union was both loving and volatile, and after Marmee's death, Louisa and her father destroyed many of Abby's journals because they were too "sad" to be left for prying eyes.

It requires only a slightly deeper probe to connect her nightmares with Louisa's admitted preference for the "lurid," if "strong and true," as she put it, using Hawthorne's *The Scarlet Letter* as her exemplar.[65] She wrote admiringly about *Anna Karenina* and the works of George Elliot; never recognizing *Little Women* as a brilliant work, she continually longed to do something "really good." She cared a great deal about *Moods,* but with many revisions, it still criss-crossed from sentimental to adventure to gothic romance in its first edition. As Nancy Bentley remarks, "rebellion is the scandal of domestic poetics."[66] During her long convalescence, Alcott wrote "A Whisper in the Dark," a chilling gothic romance in which an orphan girl is propositioned by her guardian uncle, then discovers her own mother, driven mad but still alive and shut up in the attic. Her mother warns, "Child! Woman! whatever you are, leave this accursed house while you have the power to do it."[67] She does and marries her cousin, though readers can hardly be reassured about the domestic ending, particularly since the wicked uncle-lover referred to the heroine and her mother as "a mother fiend and her daughter." Home life was the salvation of the republic, but it could also be lethally incestuous, and Alcott's gothics, often set in Europe, consistently link patriarchy, passion, and punishment.

Introduction

Moods moved between the United States, Europe, and the Caribbean, romantically racializing its heroes and heroines and dramatizing the ancient kinship ties between populations, without ever mentioning the words race, amalgamation, or miscegenation.[68] Chapter 1 begins in a room whose window fronted the west, "but a black cloud, barred with red, robbed the hour of twilight's tranquil charm." There were haunting shadows, and "Tropical luxuriance of foliage scarcely stirred by the sultry air heavy with odors that seemed to oppress not refresh." A homesick man waited for an Atlantic breeze to cheer him, and when it came, he held back "thick leaved boughs" and "chid the shrill bird beating its flame-colored breast against its prison bars." Adam Warwick, hostage to his pride and lust, has promised to marry Ottila, the "handsomest woman in Habana." Having recognized that she is "unrighteous," a "Circe" who captured his body and wants his soul as well, he tries to disengage himself, but she will not release him from his pledge. They settle on a separation for one year, during which time Ottila will try to discipline her passions and Adam will reinforce his treasured virtues: self-denial and self-help. He must leave for the North, he says, because, "This luxurious life enervates me; the pestilence of slavery lurks in the air and infects me; I must build myself up anew and find again the man I was." It is not, of course, merely the climate that saps Adam's manhood; tropical luxuriance, slave labor, and enslaving sexual passions are embodied in Ottila herself. She has a delicate face, "dark as fine bronze, a low forehead set in shadowy waves of hair, eyes full of slumberous fire, and a passionate haughty mouth that seemed shaped alike for caresses and commands." Her "black brows" contract with anger, the red mouth grows hard, her velvet cheek darkens further; she is "Delilah" and "Lola Montes," as well as "Circe." Drawing upon codes of representation so well known that they rendered "naming the race" superfluous, Alcott introduced Ottila's cousin, Andre, as "the olive-colored party," with his "swarthy face," "southern grace of manner," and Spanish accents. The cousins' manners, complexions, and their dissolution highlight the refinement and delicate sensibilities of Sylvia Yule, *Moods'* heroine, who, while dancing with Andre, becomes an even "paler blonde" as she discovers Adam Warwick's secret engagement. Adam dies, like Margaret Fuller, in a shipwreck after fighting in Italy, and Sylvia, having married a man she does not passionately love, repentantly gives up the ghost (Ottila, however, marries her cousin Andre!).

What happens when Alcott transforms a bronze-cheeked Delilah into the bronze-cheeked Apostle Paul in the story "M.L." demonstrates the problem of portraying a wounded white male body in antislavery fiction.

"M.L." was refused by the *Atlantic* in 1860, the year Alcott, at twenty-eight, finished the first draft of *Moods*.[69] The two works present striking similarities and still more significant differences, which only make sense for these products of segregated conventions delineating male and female bodies and souls. "M.L.," like its fraternal twin fiction, deals with the problem of spiritual versus bodily love and the romantic sins of jealousy, pride, lust, and envy. This story opens with a musical recital, and the sweet singer is Paul Frere. In the salon audience are "frivolous women . . . and pleasure seeking men," as well as a few more sympathetic listeners who hide their world weariness or real griefs behind "masks . . . false smiles, and vapid conversations." Momentarily, under the ministry of music, the masks fell, and "eye met eye with rare sincerity." One captivated listener is Claudia, alone in the world, "a woman of strong character and independent will, gifted with beauty, opulence and position, possessing the admiration of many, the affection of few whose love was worth desiring." Unlike Adam Warwick, Claudia does not try to "cheat her hunger into a painted feast." In short, she is chaste and reserved, and she is rewarded with Paul Frere. The setting is not Havana, but Claudia, while looking at him, remembers a painting she saw as a child, a scene almost identical to the tropical view that opens *Moods*. Once again there is "rank luxuriance" with bright-hued birds and dark shadows, "beautiful with the loom and verdure of the South." This picture, however, has a storm-wrecked grove, a thunderous cloud, and an "ominous" shipwreck. The "painting" is identical to the illustration in the Alcott family's edition of Longfellow's *Poems on Slavery* (1842). The man's face, which satisfied the eye as his voice had won Claudia's heart, had black brows "arched finely over southern eyes as full of softness as of fire." His coloring is pale bronze, and his ample black locks fall across his forehead. Like Ottila, he is in the prime of life, but his tempestuous nature has been tamed by suffering. Instead of comparisons to "Delilah," "Circe," and "Lola Montes," Paul is quickly compared to "Dante," "Saint George," and "Bruce of Scotland."

There is in this romance one softly creeping serpent or, rather, a cat named Jesse Snowden. When Jesse's attentions to Paul are rejected, she spies on the tender courtship and finds a confessional letter Paul intended for Claudia. His Southern temperament, his coloring, his air of humility, and his wounded soul have certainly, by this time, alerted the reader. Claudia, however, though she plays "Desdemona," does not suspect a Moor. On Paul's scarred right hand, the spurned Jesse reads an invisible "M.L."; the letters, Claudia soon learns from Paul, stand for "Maurice Lecroix." "Ten years ago he was my master, I his slave." The story that unfolds takes us back to Cuba, this time to meet Paul's planter father, beautiful "Quadroon" mother, and his half sister, "heiress of my father's name and fortune," Nathalie (or could she be Ottila?). Orphaned at fifteen, Paul was sold into slavery, while Nathalie went with her guardian. Paul remarks that after a few years Nathalie "had learned to look on me in another light."

Paul does not count on Claudia's sympathy at this point, much less on her love, and he begs her to understand that he was a boy—rebellious and proud—and that he had a "hard master." His recitation slips between a color-free inheritance of "high heart and eager spirit" and the European (if not quite Anglo-Saxon) blood that gave him "free instincts, aspirations, and desires." Alcott's moment of uncertainty is resolved by the iron law, "I could not change my nature though I were to be a slave forever." He ran for freedom, and hunted down, "struck a blow," and, believing himself to be dying, thought, "I am free at last." At that moment, his death might have been the only alternative in the conventional narratives of the times, had Paul been as black as Uncle Tom. The writer, a white woman, had several alternatives for ending the story of a biracial hero, however: escape and colonization, death and the salvation of a soul made white, or emancipation resulting from some combination of American Revolutionary rights and the rescue of a good woman. Alcott already had the solution in an African American's antislavery novel, William Wells Brown's *Clotel: or, the President's Daughter* (1853).[70] Like Stowe's George Harris, *Clotel*'s hero is a "white slave," and both of them rebel, escape, and "pass" into freedom with women's help. *Uncle Tom's Cabin*, however, does not suggest that Harris remain in the United States, because his Euro-American blood carries the revolutionary potential that evokes not only Concord and Lexington but also San Domingo. Alcott was also familiar with two popular plays prompted by the 1842 fugitive slave case involving George Latimer: *The Branded Hand* (1845) by Sophia L. Little and *Warren, A Tragedy* (1850) by David S. Whitney. The branded hand in the former tale prompts a slaveowner's guilty vision of mutilation, and he is converted. As a further example, Harriet Beecher Stowe's *Dred: A Tale of the Great Dismal Swamp* features Nina Gordon; mistress of her dead father's plantation, she allows her mulatto half brother to conduct her business. In Alcott's fictions, the mulatto's and, later, the mulatta's revolutionary blood is mixed with liberations sweeping across the entire world, from Concord to Paris, Rome, Warsaw, Haiti, and even, by the end of the century, to the related royalties of England and Russia, according to Margaret Fuller and the heroes of *Moods*.

Paul Frere's runaway rebellion takes place in Cuba, and he is recaptured and branded. Five years later, he climbs a balcony to his visiting sister's room, and when he looks at her "with her father's face," she offers comfort and help. She *buys* his liberty and gives him a small dowry. He then passes into the freedom of his white body, traveling through Europe and then to the United States. He explains to Claudia: "I never told my story, never betrayed my past, I have no sign of my despised race but my Spanish hue, and taking my father's native country for my own I found no bar in swarthy skin, or the only name I had a right to bear."

Paul's kindness to all women, his faith, and his "feminine" humility are the result of his gratitude to universal womanhood, embodied in the "white" sister who saved him. His only sin, then, is keeping his past and his "race" a secret from Claudia. Her sainthood is assured by her "listening to a more divine appeal, and taking counsel in the silence of her heart." She accepts him and promises to marry him; very significantly, Alcott adds one sentence that restores the sentimental racial hierarchy common to the works of antislavery white women writers: "Tears hot and heavy as a summer rain baptised the new born peace and words of broken gratitude sang its lullaby, as that strong natured cradled it with blessings and with prayers. *Paul was the weaker now,* and Claudia learned the greatness of past fear by the vehemence of present joy, as they stood together tasing the sweetness of a moment that enriched their lives."[71]

Paul's next concern is for the social isolation Claudia will endure when they marry. Claudia, however, is "fervent," a new "Maid of Orleans," and they go through with the planned large, public wedding, predictably shunned by several hundred "friends." No matter, for the two have become Christian and Christiana, and they reach the Celestial City, beckoning their false friends to make the pilgrimage and join them. Alcott's deviation from a purely conventional tale of selfhood and salvation through passive suffering is evident in her ending, a portrayal of a clearly genteel interracial marriage with children, of a circle of righteous new friends, and of Claudia: resisting the "false friends," she "only touched the little heads, looked up into her husband's face." Given the racial violence over Lincoln's election, the Emancipation Proclamation, and the escalating political struggles over miscegenation and class and gender identities, this domestic romance was a brave effort. Alcott strategically suffused the story with Christian imagery, though, unlike *Uncle Tom's Cabin,* the allusions in "M.L." were a wild confusion of historical figures and unsynchronized New Testament images.

Paul Frere's name (Brother Paul) is a broad stroke but a powerful one in several respects. The disciple Paul was born a Jew, and as a pharisee, he enforced the laws against Christ's followers until a blinding flash of light converted him on the road to Damascus and signaled his mission to the Gentiles, as well as to the Jews. He sailed to Alexandria, to Syracuse, and then to Rome itself, arguing that, although those who owned the covenant had much in their favor, the Gentiles of the world might "by nature" do the things contained in God's law, and "these having not the law, are a law unto themselves."[72] Although it is Paul Frere whom the writer compares to the peasant of Judea, preaching the sermon on the mount, his white wife, Claudia, seems to do most of the preaching to Gentiles at the end of the story. Alcott thus found a significant way to amend literary and cultural conventions that mandated representing *rebellious* black and biracial men as predatory beasts or, alternatively, portraying black or biracial men as patiently enduring earthly bondage as emasculated souls. In *Moods,* Faith Dane, a strong, moral spinster, also preaches Paul's message to Sylvia Yule, saying "You shall be a law unto yourself brave Sylvia." Alcott thereby links white women (or at least "little women") to abolition at the possible cost of regressing freedmen into childhood and the moral guardianship of abolitionist white women.

Because neither Claudia nor Faith Dane (in "The Brothers," or "My Contraband") has previously examined her own racial identity, their moments of disruptive alienation from white privilege are important. Richard Dyer explains that whiteness gains power because of its ability to "pass" as universal and invisible; it is "everything and nothing" at the same time. In "M.L.," Paul Frere's admission that he is "passing" uncovers the social construction of whiteness and blackness. Claudia's romantic love for Paul becomes "true love," in nineteenth-century feminist parlance, precisely as her racial identity (whiteness) is challenged by his revelation that he is and is not white. She uses the disruptive force of that revelation to create her own new self-identity "outside" the conventional social order; her wealth, beauty, and "whiteness," however, ensure that she is a voluntary outcast, and therefore her privilege remains intact. As Gayle Wald writes, in "White Identity in *Black Like Me*," "white sanction to 'pass' inevitably hinges on the structure of race itself, that is, on a system in which some racial identifications are more rigidly organized than others. . . . White experiments with 'blackness' are drained of their subversive potentiality . . . because they will always be recognized as experiments."[73]

Faith Dane becomes the heroine of Alcott's next antislavery romance, "The Brothers," or "My Contraband." The verbal skills of a white woman in this tale must keep a mulatto hero from killing his former master, who is, not incidentally, also his brother. The confusion over story titles reveals a tug-of-war between the white male publisher and white female writer. James Fields, editor of the *Atlantic Monthly* magazine, wanted to call it "The Brothers," but Alcott repeatedly referred to it as "My Contraband."[74] The story appeared in the *Atlantic* as "The Brothers" (November 1863), and Alcott then retitled it "My Contraband; or the Brothers" when it was reprinted in *Hospital Sketches and Camp and Fireside Stories* (Boston: Roberts Brother, 1869). The title "My Contraband" emphasizes the first-person narrative of Faith Dane, whose initial sexual attraction to the enslaved "Bob" becomes a maternal adoption of him by the end of the tale. The title "The Brothers," however, underlines the centrality of two male characters locked in incestuous rivalry, titillating readers with its suggestion of a deathly duel and possibly a transgressive black man's revenge. Fields may have won the first battle over the story's title; but Alcott clearly had a writer's edge, and the story with title insistently interposes Faith Dane between the men. Faith's first-person narrative carries an important subjective authority, supported by the content of the story.

Faith takes charge of "Bob," re-christening him "Robert" even before she hears the story of his life. His autobiography includes the well-documented horrors of incest and broken families portrayed in antislavery domestic fictions as well as in slave narratives. Faith's narration introduces the motif of a white woman's desire for a contraband hero. Nancy Bentley identified powerful boundary crossings in Richard Hildreth's *Archy Moore, The White Slave; or, Memoirs of a Fugitive,* published in 1852 and augmented in response to *Uncle Tom's Cabin* in 1856. Bentley notes, "Creating an ardent Byronic lover, Hildreth diverts the theme of love from domestic piety to the kind of narcissistic celebration of the hero's sexuality found in the poetics of high romanticism."[75] In Alcott's text, the white female narrator's aroused sensibilities seem to cross most dramatically from domestic sentiment to romance and back again. Faith Dane is powerfully attracted to her new contraband orderly:

> I had seen many contrabands, but never one so attractive as this. All colored men are called "boys" even if their heads are white; and this boy was five-and-twenty at least, strong limbed and manly, and had the look of one who never had been cowed by abuse or worn with oppressive labor.... He was more quadroon than mulatto, with Saxon features, Spanish complexion darkened by exposure, color in his lips and cheek, waving hair, and an eye full of the passionate melancholy which in such men always seems to utter a mute protest against the broken law that doomed them at their birth.

She invents a biography for him before she hears his own tale, and, imagining that he may be mourning a dead master or "a dear one still in bondage," she reaches out and touches Robert. Having evoked a domestic formula in which good women can angelically "touch" without desire, while forthrightly narrating Faith's desire, Alcott remains well within a formula fiction genre, nevertheless producing an important cultural fantasy. After the touch, "in an instant the man vanished and the slave appeared." Alcott thus insists that it is the man, tragically conscious of social boundaries and the consequences of crossing them, who forces Faith Dane to see her whiteness. Faith's sexual attraction to the "man" is immediately disarmed by his performance as the "slave," and she resumes her own mask of comforting mother and, not incidentally, her dominance. As contraband and nurse, they dance intriguingly back and forth; Bob accepts the name Robert from Faith, even as he disowns his master and father by refusing his last name. Faith's Rebel patient is, by chance, also Robert's half-brother, Master Ned; delirious with typhoid fever, he reveals the death of Robert's wife, Lucy. With that revelation, Alcott heightens the drama sexually: Robert's "strong hands closed with an ugly sort of grip," his "deep eyes filled," and his words, "My wife,—he took her—" arouse indignation, a "perfect passion of pity." Once again, Faith touches Robert; this time she "softly smoothed the long, neglected hair, pitifully wondering the while where was the wife who must have loved this tender hearted man so well."

Faith's identification with Robert's wife is transposed into the language of universal womanhood: ". . . just then I hated him [Ned] as only a woman thinking of a sister woman's wrong could hate." Again, her "I" expresses a subjectivity of the moment, a social placement experienced personally: Upon hearing the whole incestuous, brutal story of "the brothers," Faith is "hot with helpless pain and passion." Robert becomes at that moment a "universal" man, giving Faith a look "that showed no white man could have felt a deeper degradation in remembering and confessing these last acts of brotherly oppression." Robert's fratricidal rage and his experiences with being whipped and sold further South confirm that he is not, however, "white." Robert again emphasizes the boundaries between them and simultaneously exposes their hypocrisy: "Yer thought I was a white man once,—look here!" Robert tears his shirt open to show "his strong brown shoulders . . . furroughs deeply ploughed." The mutilation is as sexually arousing as it is horrifying. Faith succeeds in restraining Robert from attacking his brother only by persuading him that Lucy might still be alive and that the nurse will find out the truth.[76]

Alcott has transgressed the literary convention that usually (not always) prohibits the mutilation and public degradation of a male white slave, although she has insisted that only a white woman's weapon, "a tongue," could prevent a male "white slave" from violent revenge upon the real perpetrator of miscegenation, the white brother-rapist. Faith announces her hero's difference: "He had no religion, *for he was no saintly 'Uncle Tom'*, and Slavery's black shadow seemed to darken all the world to him, and shut out God."[77] Powerfully, she refuses to warn him of heavenly penalties or to counsel brotherly love; instead, she offers a white abolitionist's woman's "faith" that, in heaven, "where there is no black or white, no master or slave," he will surely find his Lucy. She also pragmatically stays his vengeance with the hope that Lucy may still be alive on earth. Mulattas die, fully black heroes like Uncle Tom or the unnamed "Negro" runaway in *Clotel* die in violent agonies, but, in antislavery stories by white women and white men, the male "white slave" is spared, even if, like George Harris in *Uncle Tom's Cabin,* he has to claim his African "race" and be repatriated (as Nancy Bentley has demonstrated).[78] The reader is thus prepared for the death of Robert. Faith gives Robert a Gospel and an abolitionist's lift on the Underground to Boston.

Narrative conventions did not prepare the reader for Alcott's feminist touch: Robert accepts his adoption and chooses Faith's last name as his own, but he does not join her family. In the story's first scene, "Bob" is homeless, preferring death in the street "rather than turn in with the black fellows below." Joining a black regiment as Robert Dane in a crucial "homecoming," he determines to rise with his race rather than in spite of it. He receives a death wound during the assault on Fort Wagner, a sword thrust through his chest by Captain Ned. Just vengeance is exacted when an unnamed "dark freeman" kills the Rebel and rescues "the white slave," as Alcott revealingly calls Robert in this last scene. Having moved South to teach contrabands, Faith is reunited with Robert Dane at his deathbed, saying, "my contraband found wife and home, eternal liberty and God."

Although Faith Dane has the last word, restoring her narrative authority, the Beaufort Hospital scene is quite different from the Washington opening scenes. The black regiment's white commander answers a final roll call, "Lord, here am I, with the brothers Thou hast given me." Faith Dane then envisions a new nation: "The future must show how well that fight was fought; for though Fort Wagner once defied us, public prejudice is down; and through the cannon-smoke of that black night, the manhood of the colored race shines before many eyes that would not see, rings in many ears that would not hear, wins many hearts that would not hitherto believe." The new nation is, of course, a new family in Alcott's imagery, though she leaves the problem of Southern extended families in the shadows, just as she will in "An Hour." Significantly, Robert's newest brother is the young, "dark freeman" from Boston, who "managed somehow to pitch that Reb into the fort as dead as Moses, git hold of Dane, an' bring him off." Faith Dane will presumably go on finding "dark faces" strange, missing the "sharp accent" of her Yankee boys. But the unnamed dark freeman has truly claimed Robert Dane as family, saying, "We boys always stan' by one another, an' I warn't goin' to leave him to be tormented any more by them cussed Rebs. He's been a slave once, though he don't look half so much like it as me, an' I was born in Boston."

Frederick Douglass, as Nancy Bentley observes, confirms his manhood in his 1845 and 1855 versions of *Narrative,* presenting his fight with the white overseer Covey (part of the real-life record used by Stowe in creating George Harris's rebellious moment).[79] The circumstances of writing during the Civil War privilege Alcott's representations; she is publicly a more radical writer than she could have been several years earlier, although she strategically names her abolitionist narrators as "fanatic" and yet compassionate women who will care for the enemy without loving them. Thomas Wentworth Higginson was colonel of a Negro regiment in the Union Army (First South Carolina Volunteers), and he wrote to Alcott from Beaufort about "The Brothers." In her reply, she admitted that "my contraband did not talk as he should, for even in Washington I had no time to study the genuine dialect, and when the story was written here I had no one to tell me how it should be."[80] Not able to nurse or teach in the Sea Islands of South Carolina as she had hoped, Alcott depended upon the letters of Frances Dana Barker Gage, who did visit the heroes of Fort Wagner aboard a hospital ship in Hilton Head Harbor. Rejected by the freedmen's project (a "rehearsal for reconstruction" in the form of voluntary service, funds, and supplies to freed slaves during the war), because she was an unmarried woman, Alcott asked Higginson, "Dont you want a cook, nurse or somewhat venerable 'child' for your regiment? I am willing to enlist in any capacity for the blood of old Col. May asserts itself in his granddaughter in these martial times and she is very anxious to be busied in some more loyal labor than sitting at home spinning fictions when such fine facts are waiting for all of us to profit and celebrate."[81]

There was one white hero of Fort Wagner known to Louisa Alcott personally: Sergeant Garth Wilkinson James, son of Henry James Sr. and brother to Henry and William James. She sent a copy of *Hospital Sketches* to Sergeant James, recovering from gunshot wounds, and he wrote his thanks for the "wonderful little book," which "has whiled away several otherwise weary hours and I have enjoyed reading it exceedingly."[82] Alcott's *Letters* exhibits her strategies regarding literary narrative, reveals the private liberties she took with racist jokes, and admits the professional opportunities in writing for a patriotic war market. For instance, Louisa could write to a woman friend and teacher at Frank Sanborn's school in Concord about her hospital experiences and her "boys," mentioning that one of them, with a leg amputated, had gone back to work and has "five infant cats of an Ethiopian complexion for his contrabands."[83] Perhaps the joking was prompted by Alcott's shaky recovery from typhoid fever and the public humiliation of her shaven head and skeletal appearance:

"The manliest man among my forty" was the caption to this frontispiece to *Hospital Sketches and Camp and Fireside Stories* (1869).

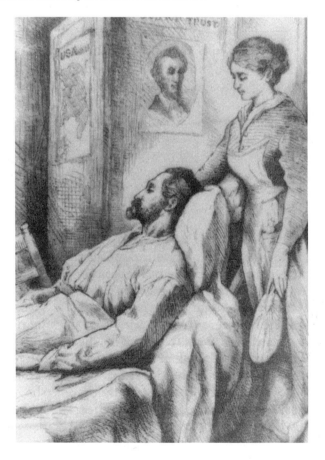

"T. Periwinkle . . . no longer wears a wig (I should say an old frisett once owned by the mother of Dr. Bellows) but appears on all occasions with a fine flowing crop."[84] She had also joked with Garth James before they were both invalids that her care package to him included a bag of nuts and apples: "The nuts are a sort of edible contraband, black, hard to take care of and not much in them in the end, but if the President cracks his nuts as thoroughly as I suspect you will these, we shall soon have you home again to play whist and sing 'Pop, pop, pop.' "[85]

By the end of the Civil War, Alcott's references to parlor games and children's songs were often made in concert with "what the little folks have done for the Sanitary Commission." Having drawn liberally, in "My Contraband," from Sanitary Commission reports and from correspondence between "colored soldiers," teachers, and relief workers, "Nelly's Hospital" duly noted the contributions of "boys and girls" to the relief work—picking lint for bandages, gathering and preserving fruits, and nursing soldiers invalided home. The heroine of the story has a brother recovering at home, and having learned about hospitals and nursing the wounded, she sets up a small animal hospital of her own with the help of the gardener's son, her mother, and Captain Will. The play hospital has all the tiny furnishings and serious practice for middle-class white women's real life that Alcott expanded memorably in the gardens and play kitchen of *Little Men*. Like *Little Women* and *Jo's Boys*,[86] this story conveys a gentle message about racial integration and social benevolence as a new nationalism. Nurse Nelly and Doctor Tony find a variety of creatures great and small to tend, including one poor fly "whose delicate wings" were caught in the net of a fat black and yellow spider. The fly buzzed and shook, struggling to free itself, but the spider had almost enshrouded its prey completely when Nurse Nelly freed the tiny creature, who lay in the palm of her hand, "faintly humming his thanks." Alcott makes the allusion quite clear:

> Nelly had heard much about contrabands, knew who they were, and was very much interested in them; so, when she freed the poor black fly, she played he was her contraband, and felt glad that her first patient was one that needed help so much. Carefully brushing away as much of the web as she could, to free his own legs, lest her clumsy fingers should hurt him; then she laid him in one of the soft beds with a grain or two of sugar . . . remembering that he was at liberty to fly away whenever he liked, because she had no wish to make a slave of him.

When the surviving volunteers made it back to Concord, as Julian Hawthorne recalled in an article in *Ladies Home Journal*, October 1922, there was "lemonade enough to flavor Walden Pond. The Alcott girls and a score more of the prettiest in the village stood in white frocks to serve out the drinks. Louisa, in her hospital costume, conducted the ceremonies." Louisa Alcott not only served as a Sanitary Commission nurse, she contributed her writing to the cause and baked, acted, and sewed for Sanitary Fairs. The United States Sanitary Commission mobilized the power of women's intelligence and their expertise, honed through decades of activity in antislavery, temperance, and benevolence. Within five days after the fall of Fort Sumter, a public meeting to organize soldiers' aid was held in Cleveland; six days later, on April 25, women assembled at the Cooper Institute in New York City and prepared an appeal to women all over the country to organize themselves in central relief associations. By early summer 1861, they addressed the secretary of war as the Women's Central Relief Association, with an advisory committee from the Board of Physicians and Surgeons of the hospitals of New York and the New York Medical Association, which furnished hospital supplies. By June the Sanitary Commission was in business as an auxiliary to the Medical Bureau and much more. Not financed by taxes or government revenue, it quickly became a gigantic charity network, staffing and supplying battlefield tents, hospitals, veterans both able and disabled as well as their families, contrabands, and war refugees. In a unique political position, the Sanitary Commission units made policies often in direct opposition to bureaucratic decisions and implemented them, sometimes with the sympathetic power of Executive Orders and army and navy personnel and sometimes against formal authorities. The mission grew until it addressed issues of pensions, the education of freedmen, women, and children, and labor negotiations for the newly freed workers. It standarized the daily living habits of soldiers and civilians, emphasizing "proper" hygiene, diets, bedding, and clothing; the volunteers, organizing themselves in businesslike (or more properly military-style) hierarchies, created local, regional, and national bureaucracies that transformed the popular concepts of nation and federal union.

Every state and regional association published regular reports and newsletters that were sent to supporters, with excerpts published in leading newspapers and magazines. Reports emphasized "facts," long lists of supplies, receipts, and "issues" for each year in each "department," a department corresponding to a military unit such as the "Department of the South, Headquarters in the Field, Morris Island, S.C." What made these "facts" so powerfully alive to readers were the firsthand accounts of conditions in each war area, and the knowledge that nurses, doctors, and other sanitary workers were the readers' kinfolk, friends, and neighbors. These reports were a modern form of journalism and an important construction of national rhetoric. Relief supplies packed by citizens of all ages in Concord, Massachusetts, would, for instance, reach the Concord volunteer company fighting the battle at Gettysburg. Louisa eagerly read and contributed writings to Sanitary Commission Reports.

The examplary report reprinted here was found in the *North American Review*, in an issue containing the work of the Reverend Theodore Parker on the abolition of slavery. The Alcott family read it, as they also read the statement of the Sanitary delegation to the secretary of war: "The present is essentially a people's war. The hearts and minds, the bodies and souls of the whole people, and of both sexes, throughout the loyal states are in it." The delegation called the war "Our second war of independence—more sacred than the first." Chapter 10 of the lengthy Commission report is representative in precisely listing the boxes of lemons, candles, tapioca, tea, and flannel bandages distributed in South Carolina in 1863, along with the ounces and pounds of quinine, morphine, and chloroform dispensed by medical officers. It is also exemplary in publicizing racial injustices and relief workers' and military efforts to remedy them. Fort Wagner and its hospital ships are described, and the plight of contrabands impressed into forced labor and women and children driven into a segregated "Camp Ethiopia" is exposed. Hospital scenes and innumerable personal stories were gathered, and white women's names and public activities became part of public culture.

Reading even a small sample of this literature reconstructs the discourses evident in Alcott's work and also reveals the audience that was momentarily sympathetic to her abolitionist, interracial stories. In the mid-nineteenth century, readers were supposed to learn proper values and how to live virtuously from their literary texts. The author was an authority, and something new emerged from Alcott's assumption of that authoritative role; women reading Louisa May Alcott's works found that she said something about their lives—she made them visible to themselves. Unquestionably, these abolitionist stories conflicted with conventional themes in many ways: Women writers and readers could always collaborate with male heroes and patriarchal cultural systems, but in this collection, including the children's story "Nelly's Hospital," the formulaic "helpmate" series became narratives of and by heroines who intelligently acted to protect and save men, reversing the romantic fairy tale expectations. Sanitary reports surely confirmed the fictions as facts.

The war had not stopped the flow of Alcott's children's stories, and it did not interfere with the market for her thrillers, although she continued carefully to separate their marketing, refusing to include sensation tales in the reprinted collections of her war stories and antislavery stories. "An Hour" precedes Alcott's thriller "Behind a Mask" by a year and seems, at first glance, to be part of a separate literary genre,[87] nevertheless, "An Hour" is an abolitionist, gothic melodrama in which the last act is better than the first, and in both stories the heroines rise from outcast status to the dignity of free womanhood. There are substantial differences, however, between Jean Muir in "Behind a Mask" and Milly in "An Hour," not the least of which proves to be the difference between race and class. Jean Muir appears as a poor white governess and is revealed to be a fallen creature, a sometime actress and a painted confidence woman "behind a mask." Admittedly, she is driven to desperate disguises because she must "marry for a living" or go on the streets once her youthful charms have faded. Given all the sympathy Alcott evokes for her plight, and because of her wit and daring, Jean Muir can and does rise as an individual, in spite of her class. In "An Hour," Alcott gets to the heart of race matters. "Milly," young, beautiful, brave, and even beloved by a wealthy, honorable young man cannot marry into upper classes "with the blood of a despised race in her veins."

"An Hour" begins as the clock strikes eleven, and in the darkness, the hero leans out a window and looks out to sea toward a coming storm; however, "neither his physical nor mental eye could see what lay before him." At midnight a daring band of fifty men and Milly herself will storm the house, kill their "masters," "do as they've been done by," and then try for liberty. Alcott slowly unfolds the title's multiple meanings: Milly, revealing the plot after she is sure that nothing can stop it, wants an hour of freedom from her "mask" of servitude. Her beauty, presumably valued because it is European, made her valuable chattel, and her virtue has been preserved only because Gabriel spared her, despite the fact that she was bought by his father to lure him into the love of slavery through a slave's lovemaking. She has pretended to be a faithful servant to her master and Gabriel's stepmother and two sisters. Still wearing her mask, she recites a list of beatings, tortures, and child sales so acceptable under slavery that her bitter recital of them draws no attention to the impending revolt or her active role in it. Milly's job is to gather weapons, destroy those she cannot take, and stop any messengers from leaving the island, thus isolating the whites. Having succeeded in doing all these tasks, Milly drops her handkerchief out the window to signal readiness, and her signal is spotted by Gabriel.

Milly is clearly mistress of the plantation now, and she will have her hour to enjoy it, with one notable distraction—Gabriel. She does love him, he does love her, and she can save him. His father is dead, and only the wicked stepmother and two wicked stepsisters remain; will the lives of three white women count for more than the lives of two hundred tortured bodies? Gabriel, in a hard-to-believe agony of indecision, finally offers himself as the sacrificial victim. Appealing to Milly and acknowledging that the whites are all in her hands now, Gabriel asks her to spare the women and prove herself a "truer woman" than they; he will free the slaves himself in the morning. Dramatically, the stepmother also bargains, promising to free Milly (alone) if she will aid their escape. Milly's words momentarily foreshadow Jean Muir: "I would not accept my liberty from you if you could give it." Alcott's careful construction of a white family that is not blood-related makes it possible for Milly and Gabriel to talk about "three white women." The suggestion of true love is thus unencumbered, and once again an interracial couple can be a "law unto themselves." Milly is, however, dissuaded from her full participation in the slaves' plot; she will save the whites for Gabriel's sake. Alcott has made his love clearly a vehicle for separating Milly from her "people" as the black soldiers in "The Brothers" named themselves: "No man had ever . . . until now recognized in her a fellow-creature, born to the same rights, gifted with the same powers, and capable of the same sufferings and sacrifices as himself. This touched and won her; that appealed to the spirit which lives through all oppression in the lowest of God's children."

Benedict Anderson reminds us that racial categories, at least since colonial America, are constructed with a "clear fiction," "that everyone has one-and-only-one extremely clear place. No fractions."[88] Milly and Gabriel are separated by "a few drops of blood," and although the heroine distinguishes between the master and the man, it is her "fraction" of color that makes her black and therefore a slave, not free to marry. The "fiction" anchors the entire system of racial slavery because mere visible distinctions of skin coloring (or other familiar traits—hair, noses, lips, and so on) might condemn a variety of individuals from any class to bondage. For this reason, miscegenation and the idea that only a "fiction" was maintaining legal systems of property and standing were "horrors." Milly could "pass" and escape with Gabriel, a model marriage such as the one in "M.L." might be presented; but "An Hour" was written and published during the Civil War, after the Emancipation Proclamation, and Gabriel also has "an hour" in which he may demonstrate the fruits of faith in God-given universal humanity. Gabriel has an hour in which voluntarily to free the slaves and save his soul (Milly has already gone off to get help and thereby save his body). In the process of saving his soul, Gabriel becomes what Alcott called, approvingly, "a womanly man."[89]

Reaching the mill house, command headquarters for the rebels, he finds the living proofs of Milly's earlier indictment of slavery. Old Cassandra, enlisted by Milly to hold off the attack until she can return with help, preaches to the assembled rebels, who are as militant and embittered as was Robert Dane when confronting his wife's rapist. Lit by the red glare of torches, having already tortured, burned, and murdered a brutal overseer, and being "of all shades of color," the rebels are led by a freeborn African, "Prince." Like Ataful in Melville's "Benito Cereno," Prince wears an iron-spiked collar fixed upon his otherwise unblemished and heroic body; he is "from one of those tribes whose wills are never broken,—who can be subdued by kindness, but who often kill themselves rather than suffer the degradation of the lash."[90] Nearby, there is another rebel, "one young man, so fair that the red lines across his shoulders looked doubly barbarous there," steadily files at the chains that bind him. Alcott suggests that another "burly brutal-looking negro" was a daunting sight because his appearance was not a natural endowment; he was "maimed and distorted by every cruelty that could be invented or inflicted."

Cassandra preaches about the heavenly deliverance awaiting all the sufferers, and finally, unheeded by those who have waited too long for "de Lord," she assures them that Gabriel will free them "to-morrer." Tomorrow, however, is still not good enough. Alcott presses home her message: Gabriel must brave the assembled armed rebels and take his chances on their mercy. Springing out like the Angel Gabriel, "out from the darkness Gabriel came among them"; ". . . this island no longer holds a master or a slave; but all are free forever and forever." As the clock strikes twelve, a "far off murmur of many voices, the tramp of many feet was heard; all knew what it protended, yet none trembled, none fled; for a mightier power than either force or fear had conquered, and the victory was already won."

Who "tramps" to the island stronghold? Could Milly have truly betrayed her brothers and sisters by bringing a slave posse? Cassandra preaches more "good news," revealing to the assembly ". . . 'bout de Norf. Its risin', boys, it's risin!—de tings we's heerd is shore, and de day ob jubilee is comin' fas'." The Union Army is advancing, and the South itself must listen to the Trumpets of Jubilee; it has "an hour" left in which to free the enslaved or face the new rebel armies. Alcott's readers never learn what happens to Milly; her future is unresolved in this narrative.

Introduction

Louisa May Alcott was a daughter of what has been called the "American Renaissance," the antebellum movement to produce a distinctive national culture. Less than a hundred years later, the "Harlem Renaissance" regionally situated another set of literary texts, transforming interracial discourses again and drawing quite differently on slave narratives, black fictions, and general codes of representation. When studying Nella Larsen's work *Passing,* I wanted to trace the history of the "tragic mulatta" trope, back perhaps to *The Tempest*.[91] I stumbled, however, attracted to the nineteenth century and my own subjective referent, the group of abolitionist tales written by Louisa May Alcott. In *Passing,* Irene Redfield, the light-skinned mulatta narrator, entertains the elite of the Harlem Renaissance at a multiracial tea party. She sees her childhood friend Clare, an exquisite, dark-eyed blonde (who has been "passing" for years), flirting with Irene's own husband, Brian, and Irene tells the reader that Clare "has a trick of sliding down ivory lids over astonishingly black eyes and then lifting them suddenly and turning on a caressing smile. Men like Dave Freeland fell for it. And Brian." Certain, at the moment, that Clare and Brian are having an affair, Irene drops and shatters a cup. In only a moment her black maid gathers up the white fragments. Protesting to a white male friend who tries to cover for her accident, Irene makes her own eye contact; she raises "innocent dark eyes to his concerned pale ones," and says:

> Did you notice that cup? Well you're lucky. It was the ugliest thing that your ancestors the charming Confederates ever owned. I've forgotten how many thousand of years ago it was that Brian's great great grand uncle owned it. But it has, or had a good old hoary history. It was brought North by way of the subway. Oh, all right. Be English if you want to and call it the underground. What I'm coming to is the fact that I've never figured out a way of getting rid of it until about five minutes ago. I had an inspiration. I had only to break it, and I was rid of it for ever. So simple. And, I'd never thought of it before.[92]

This social lie, of course, masks a deeper national denial of miscegenation—the fear of a future that has already happened. Irene's troubles, and Brian's and Clare's, are embodied in the rule "no fractions" and in the fiction of clear, fixed racial (and sexual) categories. The small and troubling questions that connect "An Hour" and *Passing* over all the years are: What happened to Milly? Where did she go? and, where did that ugly "Confederate" teacup originate, or Who are Brian Redfield's great-great-granduncle and -aunt? Is it possible that Milly, a light-skinned woman, "passed" as she traveled North carrying in a carpetbag a few pieces of clothing and cast-off utensils, among them, a china teacup? Could Milly and even Gabriel be Brian Redmond's ancestors? Judith Butler read Larsen's 1929 tale and forwarded the broken teacup motif to Toni Morrison's *Sula,* suggesting that "We might read . . . *Sula* as the piecing together of the shattered whiteness that composed the remains of both Clare and Irene in Nella Larsen's text." Butler sees Clare in Sula and Irene in Nel, refiguring their rivalries as the recognition of sisterhood in Nel's final call: "girl, girl, girlfriend."[93] Alcott's fiction allowed for only one mulatta heroine, who must choose between saving a white man and carrying out a slave rebellion. "An Hour" ends with a menacing challenge to the slaveholding South: End slavery, grant citizenship to subjects, and the national family may be reconstructed. Perhaps Louisa May Alcott, in spite of Faith Dane's identification with a "sister woman," could not write beyond her ending.

NOTES

1. John Limon, *Writing After War, American War Fiction From Realism to Postmodernism* (New York, 1994) p. 183. James Wallace argues that the Civil-War provided Alcott with "the means to satisfy both her readers' expectations and her own ambitions for her heroine" in her *Work, A Story of Experience* (Boston, 1873); Wallace, "Where the Absent Father Went," in *Refiguring the Father: New Feminist Readings of Patriarchy,* ed. Patricia Yaeger and Beth Kowalski Wallace (Carbondale, Ill., 1989) p. 268.

2. Louisa May Alcott in *Hospital Sketches* (Boston, 1863) has her alter ego, Nurse Tribulation Periwinkle, refer to herself as a "fanatic" for the cause of abolition. In *The Wages of Whiteness: Race and the Making of the American Working Class* (London, 1991) David Roediger argues that the 1834 New York City race and anti-abolitionist riots "also featured white workers seeking to protect 'their women' . . . but from amalgamation with Blacks, not with the wealthy" (p. 108). By the latter stages of the Civil War, however, he notes that workers sang "John Brown's Body" as a "labor anthem."

3. Louisa May Alcott, *Little Women* (New York, Modern Library edition, 1983), Chapter 24, "Harvest Time."

4. Cynthia H. Barton, *Transcendental Wife, The Life of Abigail May Alcott* (Lanham, Md., 1996), p. 152.

5. Ednah Dow Cheney, ed., *Louisa May Alcott: Life, Letters and Journals* (Boston, 1928), p. 120.

6. Alcott, *Hospital Sketches.*

7. Louisa May Alcott, "Colored Soldiers' Letters," *Commonwealth* 25, no. 44 (July 1, 1864); reprinted here for the first time. "An Hour," *Commonwealth*

3, nos. 13, 14 (Nov. 26, Dec. 3, 1864); reprinted in *Camp and Fireside Stories* (Boston, 1869).

8. Elizabeth Young, "A Wound of One's Own: Louisa May Alcott's Civil War Fiction," *American Quarterly* 48, no. 3 (September 1996), p. 443. Speaking of *Hospital Sketches*, Young says, "In Alcott's metaphorical translation of female traits into male bodies, the best man in the wake of battle behaves like a woman. At the same time, in an apparent reversal of this feminization, Alcott also suggests that the best woman for the hospital is surprisingly like a man." Nurse Periwinkle's maternal performance reveals that femininity is "unstable" rather than being an innate identity. Alcott's war writings cannot heal the "wound" of femininity, "but at least the terms of such wounding could be altered and valorized. Alcott . . . rewrites the woman writer's quest for a room of one's own into the double-edged desire—at once rebellious and self-regulating—for a wound of one's own" (p. 443).

9. Biographical details for the extended May-Alcott family are drawn from Madelon Bedell, *The Alcotts, Biography of a Family* (New York, 1980); Madeleine B. Stern, *Louisa May Alcott* (New York, 1995); Barton, *Transcendental Wife;* and Sarah Elbert, *A Hunger for Home: Louisa May Alcott's Place in American Culture* (New Brunswick, N.J., 1987).

10. Margaret Fuller, *Woman in the Nineteenth Century and Other Kindred Papers by Margaret Fuller Ossoli,* ed. Arthur Buckminster Fuller (Boston, 1855).

11. Abigail May Alcott, *Journal,* January 1, 1836, *Memoir* (transcribed by Bronson Alcott), 1878, Houghton Library, Harvard University.

12. Ralph Waldo Emerson, *Essays,* First Series, published as "History," "Self-Reliance," "Compensation," "Spiritual Laws," "Love," "Friendship," "Prudence," "Heroism," "The Over-Soul," "Circles," "Intellect," "Art" (Boston, 1841). I have relied here on Stephen E. Whicher, *Freedom and Fate, An Inner Life of Ralph Waldo Emerson* (New York, 1961).

13. David Walker, cited in Herbert Aptheker, *"One Continual Cry," David Walker's Appeal* (New York, 1965), p. 54.

14. Cited in Bedell, p. 103. See also Roediger, *Wages of Whiteness,* pp. 86–87.

15. Samuel J. May, cited in Catherine Covert Stepanek, "Saint Before His Time: Samuel J. May and American Educational Reform" (master's thesis, Syracuse University, 1967), p. 11.

16. Leonard Richards, *"Gentlemen of Property and Standing": Anti-Abolition Mobs in Jacksonian America* (London, Oxford, New York, 1970), p. 43.

17. The quotation from the *New York Times* and the connections among abolition, amalgamation, and middle-class romance are discussed in Elise Virginia Lemire, "Making Miscegenation: Discourses of Interracial Sex and Mar-

riage in the United States, 1790–1865" (Ph.D. dissertation, Rutgers, State University of New Jersey, 1996), p. 51. I am grateful to Professor Lemire for generously sharing her manuscript with me; her powerful treatment of texts and historical contexts includes an overview of recent scholarship on the production of "amalgamation" and miscegenation." See also Bedell, *The Alcotts,* p. 106, for Harriet Martineau's refusal to condemn "amalgamation."

18. Lemire, "Making Miscegenation."

19. Bedell, *The Alcotts,* p. 24.

20. Odell Shephard, ed., *The Journals of Bronson Alcott* (Boston, 1938), p. 173.

21. Louisa May Alcott, *Moods* (Boston, 1864). The relationship between the Alcotts' radical abolitionism and the European revolutions of 1848 is illuminated by Larry J. Reynolds's fine work, *European Revolutions and the American Literary Renaissance* (New Haven, 1988). See also Bell Gale Chevigny, *The Woman and the Myth: Margaret Fuller's Life and Writings* (New York, 1976; revised ed. Boston, 1994), and an earlier discovery of Leona Rostenberg, "Mazzini to Margaret Fuller, 1847–1849," *American Historical Review* 47 (October 1941).

22. Louisa May Alcott, "Transcendental Wild Oats," *The Independent* 25, no. 1307 (Dec. 18, 1873).

23. Cited in Shephard, *Journals,* pp. 193–94.

24. Cited in Bedell, *The Alcotts,* p. 262.

25. Cited in Reynolds, *European Revolutions,* p. 30. Reynolds shows that Emerson reconsidered his early distaste for European revolutionaries after witnessing the "fire and fury" of the radicals. Writing home to his wife, he admitted that "the deep sincerity of the speakers who are agitating social not political questions and who are studying how to secure a fair share of bread to every man, and to get the God's justice done through the land, is very good to hear" (p. 34). See also Joel Porte, *Emerson and Thoreau: Transcendentalists in Conflict* (Middletown, 1964).

26. Cited in Reynolds, *European Revolutions,* p. 55.

27. Ibid., p. 58.

28. Ibid., p. 62.

29. Ibid., p. 75.

30. Cited in Bedell, *The Alcotts,* p. 328.

31. Reverend Theodore Parker was the most important religious influence (next to her uncle, the Reverend Samuel J. May) in Louisa May Alcott's life. As a close family friend, he counseled and found work for Louisa when she was out of work and most desperately poor. An abolitionist and an ardent supporter of the rights of women and the "laboring classes," his thoughts on the

relationship of nations and races seem to be similar to the paradoxes that gripped Alcott. Parker died young, and Alcott later favored institutional "education" of "lesser" groups; the friends believed in both science and spirituality. I am grateful to historian Dean Grodzins, Harvard University, for sharing his paper on Parker, "Matter, Spirit, and Transcendental Racial Theory," part of a stimulating original analysis.

32. Thomas Wentworth Higginson, *Cheerful Yesterdays* (Boston, 1898), pp. 157, 158.

33. Louisa May Alcott, "The Rival Painters. A Tale of Rome," *Olive Branch* 17, no. 19 (May 8, 1852).

34. Madeleine B. Stern, ed., *Louisa May Alcott Unmasked, Collected Thrillers* (Boston, 1995).

35. Cited in Lemire, "Making Miscegenation," p. 205.

36. Abraham Lincoln, *Speeches and Writings, 1832–1858* (New York, 1989), pp. 397–98.

37. See George M. Fredrickson, *The Black Image in the White Mind: The Debate on Afro-American Character and Destiny, 1817–1914* (New York, 1971); Martha Hodes, "Wartime Dialogues on Illicit Sex: White Women and Black Men," in *Divided Houses: Gender and the Civil War,* ed. Catherine Clinton and Nina Silber (New York, 1992); and Lemire, "Making Miscegenation."

38. Susan Gillman, "The Mulatto, Tragic or Triumphant? The Nineteenth-Century American Race Melodrama," in *The Culture of Sentiment,* ed. Shirley Samuels (New York, 1992), pp. 224–25.

39. Elbert, *A Hunger for Home,* p. 145.

40. Ibid., p. 146.

41. Alcott, *Work,* Chapter 2, "Servant." Christie Devon, the heroine, is told, "My Cook is black." Christie replies, "I have no objection to color, ma'am." Alcott then writes, "An expression of relief dawned upon Mrs. Stuart's countenance, for the black cook had been an insurmountable obstacle to all the Irish ladies who had applied." See Roediger, *Wages of Whiteness,* and Grodzins, "Matter, Spirit, and Transcendental Racial Theory," on the issue. Margaret Higonnet provides an interesting discussion of *Work* and civil wars on "home territory" in "Civil Wars and Sexual Territories," in *Arms and the Woman,* ed. Helen Cooper, Adrienne Munich, and Susan Squier (Chapel Hill, N.C., 1989).

42. Alcott, *Moods.*

43. Louisa May Alcott to Alfred Whitman, March 2, 1860, Houghton Library, Harvard University, reprinted in *The Selected Letters of Louisa May Alcott,* ed. Joel Myerson, Daniel Shealy, and Madeleine B. Stern (Boston, 1987), pp. 51, 52.

44. Elbert, *A Hunger for Home,* p. 151.

45. Ibid., p. 153.

46. Alcott, *Hospital Sketches*, p. 75.

47. Cheney, *Alcott*, pp. 117, 118.

48. Ibid., p. 118.

49. Ibid.

50. Alcott, *Hospital Sketches*, p. 51. For an illuminating reading of *Hospital Sketches*, see Young, "A Wound of Her Own."

51. Elbert, *A Hunger for Home*, p. 155.

52. Ibid.

53. Cheney, *Alcott*, p. 119 (Jan. 21, 1864).

54. Cited and discussed in Sidney Kaplan, "The Miscegenation Issue in the Election of 1864," *Journal of Negro History* 31 (July 1949), pp. 274–343. See Roediger, *Wages of Whiteness*, and Lemire, "Making Miscegenation," for the most compelling recent studies, especially Lemire, Chapter 5, "The Invention of Miscegenation."

55. Stern, *Louisa May Alcott Unmasked*, Introduction.

56. Cited in Lemire, "Making Miscegenation," p. 214.

57. Ibid., p. 216.

58. *Commonwealth* 1, no. 24 (Jan. 24, 1863).

59. Ibid., 1, no. 25.

60. Elbert, *A Hunger for Home*, p. 156. See David Brion Davis, *Slavery and Human Progress* (New York, 1984).

61. Lora Romero, "Vanishing Americans: Gender, Empire, and New Historicism," in *Subjects and Citizens: Nation, Race and Gender from Oroonoko to Anita Hill*, ed. Michael Moon and Cathy N. Davidson (Durham and London, 1995), pp. 87–108. This entire volume is exceptionally useful in framing studies of race, gender, and American literary studies.

62. Ibid.

63. Ibid.

64. Ibid. Romero refers to Michael Foucault, *The History of Sexuality, Vol. I: An Introduction*, trans. Robert Hurley (New York, 1980).

65. "The Scarlet Letter is my favorite. Mother likes Mrs. B [Frederika Bremmer] better, as more wholesome. I fancy 'lurid things' if true and strong also." Cheney, *Alcott*, p. 36.

66. Nancy Bentley, "White Slaves: The Mulatto Hero in Antebellum Fiction," in *Subjects and Citizens*, ed. Moon and Davidson, pp. 195–216. Romero and Bentley argue for the importance of gendered bodies in antislavery fiction, as well as for the significance of the author's gender and race.

67. Louisa May Alcott, "A Whisper in the Dark," *Frank Leslie's Illustrated*

Newspaper, 16, nos. 401 and 402 (June 6 and 13, 1863). Elizabeth Keyser, *Whisper in the Dark: The Fiction of Louisa May Alcott* (Knoxville, Tenn., 1993).

68. Alcott, *Moods,* chapter 1.

69. Elbert, *A Hunger for Home,* pp. 116–17.

70. William Wells Brown, *Clotel: or, the President's Daughter* (1853). For discussions of the mulatta traditions see Sterling A. Brown, *The Negro in American Fiction* (Washington, D.C., 1938); Carolyn Karcher, "Rape, Murder and Revenge in 'Slavery's Pleasant Homes'; Lydia Maria Child's Antislavery Fiction and the Limits of Genre," *Women's Studies International Forum* 9 (Fall 1986) and Bentley, "White Slaves."

71. Emphasis mine.

72. The Epistle of Paul the Apostle to the Romans, 2:14. My thanks to Professor Richard Dalfiume for our discussions on Romans.

73. Alcott, *Moods,* Chapter 18. Richard Dyer, "White," *Screen* 29, no. 3 (1988), pp. 44–64, cited in Gayle Wald, "White Identity in *Black Like Me*," in *Passing and the Fictions of Identity,* ed. Elaine K. Ginsberg (Durham and London, 1996), pp. 162–63.

74. Louisa May Alcott to James Redpath, Sept. 29, 1863, reprinted in Myerson et al., *Selected Letters,* pp. 93, 94. General Benjamin Butler designated escaped slaves as "contraband" or "spoils of war" who did not have to be returned to their masters.

75. For the conventions of the mulatto as "white body" and also the possibilities of violent resistance by "white slaves," black slaves, and mulatto slaves, see Bentley, "White Slaves," pp. 195–216.

76. Alcott's presentation of a young, half-naked mulatto hero locking the door in a room with a sympathetic white woman and his wounded white brother has several possible readings. I see it as a transgressive or disruptive movement for both Robert and Faith Dane. Kathleen Diffley agrees that the scene is significant for both characters but offers an illuminating reading of this scene as representative of the "Old Homestead" narrative with a difference. Robert Dane enlists in the Fifty-Fourth Massachusetts regiments, replacing "Miss Dane as the narrative's primary mover"; he wins "a place in the national household." Kathleen Diffley, *Where My Heart Is Turning Ever: Civil War Stories and Constitutional Reform, 1861–1876* (Athens, Ga., 1992), p. 37.

77. Emphasis mine.

78. Bentley, "White Slaves," p. 213, refers to this alternative as "the geographical relocation of slaves by a black nationalist (George Harris)."

79. Ibid.

80. Louisa May Alcott to Thomas Wentworth Higginson, Nov. 12, 1863, reprinted in Myerson et al., *Selected Letters,* pp. 96, 97.

81. Ibid.

82. Garth Wilkinson James to Louisa May Alcott, cited in Myerson et al., *Selected Letters*, p. 94.

83. Louisa May Alcott to Mary Elizabeth Waterman, Nov. 6, 1863, reprinted in Myerson et al., *Selected Letters*, pp. 94, 95.

84. Ibid.

85. Louisa May Alcott to Edward J. Bartlett and Garth Wilkinson James, Dec. 4, 1862, reprinted in Myerson et al., *Selected Letters*, pp. 81, 82.

86. Louisa May Alcott, *Little Men: Life at Plumfield with Jo's Boys* (Boston, 1871), Chapter 5, "Patty Pans."

87. Louisa May Alcott, "Behind a Mask: or, A Woman's Power," *The Flag of Our Union* 21, nos. 41, 42, 43, 44 (Oct. 13, 20, 27, and Nov. 3, 1866); reprinted in Stern, *Louisa May Alcott Unmasked*. See Judith Fetterly, "Impersonating 'Little Women': The Radicalism of Alcott's Behind a Mask," *Journal of Women's Studies* 10 (1983) pp. 1–14.

88. Benedict Anderson, *Imagined Communities: Reflections on the Origin and Spread of Nationalism*, rev. ed. (London, New York, 1991). I am grateful to students in my Nineteenth-Century U.S. History and Literature class (Spring 1996) at Binghamton University for this insight and reference. Lemire notes the same source, amplifying Anderson's comments on the census.

89. In a December 26, 1862, letter to her friend the veteran nurse Hannah Stevenson, to whom Louisa May Alcott dedicated *Hospital Sketches*, Alcott, nursing at the Union Hotel Hospital, expressed an "all pervading bewilderment" at having to "wash and put clean clothes on some eight or ten dreary faced, dirty and wounded men." She "proceeded to do it very much as I should have attempted to cut off arms or legs if ordered to. Having no brothers and a womanly man for a father I find myself rather staggered by some of the performances about me but possessing a touch of Macawber's spirt—I still hope to get used to it and hold myself ready for a spring if anything turns up." In this same letter Alcott describes herself as haunting the ward at night "like a stout brown ghost." This frank, self-conscious confidence was recently located at the Massachusetts Historical Society, in the Curtis-Stevenson Family Papers. The full text is published in *MHS Miscellany*, no. 65 (Fall 1996).

90. Herman Melville, "Benito Cereno" (1855), in *Benito Cereno, Great Short Works of Herman Melville*, ed. Warner Berthoff (New York, 1969). For a full historical and literary analysis, see Eric J. Sundquist, "Benito Cereno and New World Slavery," in *Reconstructing American Literary History*, ed. Sacvan Bercovitch (Cambridge, 1986).

91. Nella Larsen, *Quicksand and Passing*, reprint, ed. Deborah E. McDowell (New Brunswick, N.J., 1986).

92. Larsen, *Passing,* Chapter 3.

93. Judith Butler, *Bodies That Matter,* Chapter 6, "Passing, Queering: Nella Larsen's Psychoanalytic Challenge," p. 183. I am grateful to Professor Susan Belasco Smith, Gus Stadler, Professor Nancy Henry, and the Alcott Society session at the American Literature Association Conference on American Literature, San Diego, 1996, and to Mary V. Dougherty, of the English Department at Rutgers University, for her insightful analyses in "Louisa May Alcott's Maternalism" and "Contraband Desire."

Louisa May Alcott

ON RACE, SEX, AND SLAVERY

M . L .

CHAPTER I

"The sun set—but not his hope:
Stars rose—his face was earlier up:
He spoke, and words more soft than rain
Brought back the Age of Gold again:
His action won such reverence sweet,
As hid all measure of the feat."

*H*U S H ! let me listen."

Mrs. Snowden ceased her lively gossip, obedient to the command, and leaning her head upon her hand, Claudia sat silent.

Like a breath of purer air, the music floated through the room, bringing an exquisite delight to the gifted few, and stirring the dullest nature with a sense of something nobler than it knew. Frivolous women listened mutely, pleasure-seeking men confessed its charm, world-worn spirits lived again the better moments of their lives, and wounded hearts found in it a brief solace for the griefs so jealously concealed. At its magic touch the masks fell from many faces and a momentary softness made them fair, eye met eye with rare sincerity, false smiles faded, vapid conversation died abashed, and for a little space, Music, the divine enchantress, asserted her supremacy, wooing tenderly as any woman, ruling royally as any queen.

Like water in a desert place, Claudia's thirsty spirit drank in the silver sounds that fed her ear, and through the hush they came to her like a remembered strain. Their varying power swayed her like a wizard's wand, its subtle softness wrapped her senses in a blissful calm, its passion thrilled along her nerves like south winds full of an aroma fiery and sweet, its energy stirred her blood like martial music or heroic speech,—for this

Originally published in the *Commonwealth* 1, nos. 21, 22, 23, 24, 25 (January 24, 31, and February 7, 14, 21, 1863). Reprinted in *Journal of Negro History* 14, no. 4 (October 1929).

mellow voice seemed to bring her the low sigh of pines, the ardent breath of human lips, the grand anthem of the sea. It held her fast, and lifting her above the narrow bounds of time and place, blessed her with a loftier mood than she had ever known before, for midsummer night and warmth seemed born of it, and her solitary nature yearned to greet the genial influence as frost-bound grasses spring to meet the sun.

What the song was, she never heard, she never cared to know; to other ears it might be love-lay, barcarole, or miserere for the dead,—to her it was a melody devout and sweet as saintliest hymn, for it had touched the chords of that diviner self whose aspirations are the flowers of life, it had soothed the secret pain of a proud spirit, it had stirred the waters of a lonely heart, and from their depths a new born patience rose with healing on its wings.

Silent she sat, one hand above her eyes, the other lying in her lap, unmoved since with her last words it rose and fell. The singer had been forgotten in the song, but as the music with triumphant swell soared upward and grew still, the spell was broken, the tide of conversation flowed again, and with an impatient sigh, Claudia looked up and saw her happy dream depart.

"Who is this man? you told me but I did not hear."

With the eagerness of a born gossip, Mrs. Snowden whispered the tale a second time in her friend's ear.

"This man (as you would never call him had you seen him) is a Spaniard, and of noble family, I'm sure, though he denies it. He is poor, of course,—these interesting exiles always are,—he teaches music, and though an accomplished gentleman and as proud as if the 'blue blood' of all the grandees of Spain flowed in his veins, he will not own to any rank, but steadily asserts that he is 'plain Paul Frere, trying honestly to earn his bread, and nothing more.' Ah, you like that, and the very thing that disappoints me most, will make the man a hero in your eyes."

"Honesty is an heroic virtue, and I honor it wherever it is found. What further, Jessie?" and Claudia looked a shade more interested than when the chat began.

"Only that in addition to his charming voice, he is a handsome soul, beside whom our pale-faced gentlemen look boyish and insipid to a mortifying degree. Endless romances are in progress, of which he may be the hero if he will, but unfortunately for his fair pupils the fine eyes of their master seem blind to any 'tremolo movements' but those set down in the book; and he hears them warble *'O mio Fernando'* in the tenderest of spoken languages as tranquilly as if it were a nursery song. He leads a solitary

life, devoted to his books and art, and rarely mixes in the society of which
I think him a great ornament. This is all I know concerning him, and if
you ever care to descend from your Mont Blanc of cool indifference, I
fancy this minstrel will pay you for the effort. Look! that is he, the dark
man with the melancholy eyes; deign to give me your opinion of my
modern 'Thaddeus.'"

Claudia looked well, and, as she did so, vividly before her mind's eye
rose a picture she had often pondered over when a child.

A painting of a tropical island, beautiful with the bloom and verdure of
the South. An ardent sky, flushed with sunrise canopied the scene, palm
trees lifted their crowned heads far into the fervid air, orange groves
dropped dark shadows on the sward where flowers in rank luxuriance
glowed like spires of flame, or shone like stars among the green. Bright-
hued birds swung on vine and bough, dainty gazelles lifted their human
eyes to greet the sun, and a summer sea seemed to flow low—singing to
the bloomy shore. The first blush and dewiness of dawn lay over the still
spot, but looking nearer, the eye saw that the palm's green crowns were
rent, the vines hung torn as if by ruthless gusts, and the orange boughs
were robbed of half their wealth, for fruit and flowers lay thick upon the
sodden earth. Far on the horizon's edge, a thunderous cloud seemed rolling westward, and on the waves an ominous wreck swayed with the sway-
ing of the treacherous sea.

Claudia saw a face that satisfied her eye as the voice had done her ear,
and yet its comeliness was not its charm. Black locks streaked an ample
forehead, black brows arched finely over southern eyes as full of softness
as of fire. No color marred the pale bronze of the cheek, no beard hid the
firm contour of the lips, no unmeaning smile destroyed the dignity of a
thoughtful countenance, on which nature's hand had set the seal wherewith she stamps the manhood that no art can counterfeit.

But as she searched it deeper, Claudia saw upon the forehead lines that
seldom come to men of thirty, in the eye the shadow of some past despair,
and about the closely folded lips traces of an impetuous nature tamed by
suffering and taught by time. Here, as in the picture, the tempest seemed
to have gone by, but though a gracious day had come, the cloud had left
a shade behind. Sweet winds came wooingly from off the shore, and the
sea serenely smiled above the wreck, but a vague unrest still stirred the
air, and an undertone of human woe still whispered through the surges'
song.

"So Dante might have looked before his genius changed the crown of thorns into a crown of roses for the woman he loved," thought Claudia, then said aloud in answer to her friend's last words,

"Yes, I like that face, less for its beauty than its strength. I like that austere simplicity of dress, that fine unconsciousness of self, and more than all I like the courtesy with which he listens to the poorest, plainest, least attractive woman in the room. Laugh, if you will, Jessie, I respect him more for his kindness to neglected Mary Low, than if for a fairer woman he had fought as many battles as Saint George. This is true courtesy, and it is the want of this reverence for womanhood in itself, which makes many of our so-called gentlemen what they are, and robs them of one attribute of real manliness."

"Heaven defend us! here is an Alpine avalanche of praise from our Diana! Come, be made known to this Endymion before you can congeal again," cried Jessie; for Claudia's words were full of energy, and in her eye shone an interest that softened its cold brilliancy and gave her countenance the warmth which was the charm it needed most. Claudia went, and soon found herself enjoying the delights of conversation in the finer sense of that word. Paul Frere did not offer her the stale compliments men usually think it proper to bestow upon a woman, as if her mind were like a dainty purse too limited for any small coin of any worth, nor did he offer her the witty gossips current in society, which, like crisp bank bills, rustle pleasantly, and are accepted as a "counterfeit presentiment," of that silver speech, which should marry sound to sense. He gave her sterling gold, that rang true to the ear, and bore the stamp of genuine belief, for unconsciously he put himself into his words, and made them what they should be,—the interpreters of one frank nature to another.

He took the few pale phantoms custom has condemned to serve as subjects of discourse between a man and a woman in a place like that, and giving them vitality and color, they became the actors of his thought, and made a living drama of that little hour. Yet he was no scholar erudite and polished by long study or generous culture. Adversity had been his college, experience his tutor, and life the book whose lessons stern and salutary he had learned with patient pain. Real wrong and suffering and want had given him a knowledge no philosopher could teach, real danger and desolation had lifted him above the petty fears that take the heroism out of daily life, and a fiery baptism had consecrated heart and mind and soul to one great aim, beside which other men's ambitions seemed most poor. This was the secret charm he owned, this gave the simplicity that dignified his manner, the sincerity that won in his address; this proved the supremacy of character over culture, opulence and rank, and made him what he was—a man to command respect and confidence and love.

Dimly Claudia saw, and vaguely felt all this in that brief interview; but when it ended, she wished it were to come again, and felt as if she had left the glare and glitter of the stage whereon she played her part, for a moment had put off her mask to sit down in the ruddy circle of a household fire where little shadows danced upon the walls, and tender tones made common speech divine.

"It will be gone tomorrow, this pleasure beautiful and brief, and I shall fall back into my old disappointment again, as I have always done before"; she sighed within herself. Yet when she sat alone in her own home, it seemed no longer solitary, and like a happy child she lulled herself to sleep with fitful snatches of a song she had never heard but once.

CHAPTER II

Claudia stood alone in the world, a woman of strong character and independent will, gifted with beauty, opulence and position, possessing the admiration and esteem of many, the affection of a few whose love was worth desiring. All these good gifts were hers, and yet she was not satisfied. Home ties she had never known, mother-love had only blessed her long enough to make its loss most keenly felt, the sweet confidence of sisterhood had never warmed her with its innocent delights, "father" and "brother" were unknown words upon her lips, for she had never known the beauty and the strength of man's most sincere affection.

Many hands had knocked at the closed door, but knocked in vain, for the master had not come, and true to her finer instincts, Claudia would not make a worldly marriage or try to cheat her hunger into a painted feast. She would have all or nothing, and when friends urged or lovers pleaded, she answered steadily:

"I cannot act a lie, and receive where I have nothing to bestow. If I am to know the blessedness of love, it will come to me, and I can wait."

Love repaid her loyalty at last. Through the close-scented air of the conservatory where she had lived a solitary plant, there came a new influence, like a breath of ocean air, both strengthening and sweet. Then the past ceased to be a mournful memory; for over her lost hopes, the morning glories that had early died,—over her eager desires, the roses that had never bloomed—over broken friendships, the nests whence all the birds were flown—a pleasant twilight seemed to fall, and across the sombre present came the ruddy herald of a future dawn. It brought the magic moment when the flower could bloom, the master's hand whose touch unbarred the door, the charmed voice that woke the sleeping princess, and sang to her of

"That new world, which is the old".

In "plain Paul Frere," Claudia found her hero, recognized her king, although like Bruce he came in minstrel guise and accepted royally the alms bestowed.

Slowly, by rare interviews, the swift language of the eye, and music's many wiles, Paul caught deeper glimpses into Claudia's solitary life, and felt the charm of an earnest nature shining through the maidenly reserve that veiled it from his search. He sang to her, and singing, watched the still fire that kindled in her eye, the content that touched her lips with something softer than a smile, the warmth that stole so beautifully to her face, melting the pride that chilled it, banishing the weariness that saddened it, and filling it with light, and hope, and bloom, as if at his command the woman's sorrows fell away and left a happy girl again. It was a dangerous power to wield, but with the consciousness of its possession came a sentiment that curbed a strong man's love of power, and left the subject to a just man's love of right.

He denied himself the happiness of ministering to Claudia the frequent feasts she loved, for it was offering her a wine more subtle than she knew, a wine whose potency her friend already felt. He seldom sang to her alone, but conversation was a rich reward for this renunciation, for in those hours, beautiful and brief, he found an interest that "grew by what it fed on," and soon felt that it was fast becoming sweeter to receive than to bestow.

Claudia was a student of like dangerous lore, for she too scanned her new friend warily and well; often with keen perceptions divining what she dared not seek, with swift instincts feeling what she could not see. Her first judgments had been just, her first impressions never changed. For each month of increasing friendship, was one of increasing honor and esteem.

This man who earned his bread, and asked no favors where he might have demanded many, who would accept no fictitious rank, listen to no flattering romance, who bore the traces of a fateful past, yet showed no bitterness of spirit, but went his way steadfastly, living to some high end unseen by human eyes, yet all-sustaining in itself,—this man seemed to Claudia the friend she had desired, for here she found a character built up by suffering and time, an eager intellect aspiring for the true, and valiant spirit looking straight and strong into the world.

To her ear the music of his life became more beautiful than any lay he sang, and on his shield her heart inscribed the fine old lines,

"Lord of himself, though not of lands,
And having nothing, yet hath all."

CHAPTER III

One balmy night, when early flowers were blossoming in Claudia's garden, and the west wind was the almoner of their sweet charities, she sat looking with thoughtful eyes into the shadowy stillness of the hour.

Miss Blank, the mild nonentity who played propriety in Claudia's house, had been absorbed into the darkness of an inner room, where sleep might descend upon her weary eyelids without an open breach of that decorum which was the good soul's staff of life.

Paul Frere, leaning in the shadow, looked down upon the bent head whereon the May moon dropped a shining benediction; and as he looked, his countenance grew young again with hope, and fervent with strong desire. Silence had fallen on them, for watching *her,* Paul forgot to speak, and Claudia was plucking leaf after leaf from a flower that had strayed from among the knot that graced her breast. One by one the crimson petals fluttered to the ground, and as she saw them fall a melancholy shadow swept across her face.

"What has the rose done that its life should be so short?" her friend asked as the last leaf left her hand.

As if the words recalled her to the present, Claudia looked at the dismantled stem, saying regretfully, "I forgot the flower, and now I have destroyed it with no skill to make it live again." She paused a moment, then added smiling as if at her own fancies, though the regretful cadence lingered in her voice, "This is my birth-night, and thinking of my past, the rose ceased to be a rose to me, and became a little symbol of my life. Each leaf I gathered seemed a year, and as it fell I thought how fast, how vainly, they had gone. They should have been fairer in aspirations, fuller of duties, richer in good deeds, happier in those hopes that make existence sweet, but now it is too late. Poor rose! Poor life!" and from the smiling lips there fell a sigh.

Paul took the relic of the rose, and with a gesture soft as a caress, broke from the stem a little bud just springing from its mossy sheath, saying with a glance as full of cheer as hers had been of despondency, "My friend, it never is too late. Out of the loneliest life may bloom a higher beauty than the lost rose knew. Let the first sanguine petals fall, their perfume will remain a pleasant memory when they are dead; but cherish the fairer flower that comes so late, nurture it with sunshine, baptise it with dew, and though the garden never knows it more, it may make summer in some shady spot and bless a household with its breath and bloom. I have no gift wherewith to celebrate this night, but let me give you back a happier emblem of the life to be, and with it a prophecy that when another six and twenty years are gone, no sigh will mar your smile as you look back and say, 'Fair rose! Fair life!'"

Claudia looked up with traitorous eyes, and answered softly—"I accept the prophecy, and will fulfil it, if the black frost does not fall." Then with a wistful glance and all persuasive tone, she added, "You have forgotten one gift always in your power to bestow. Give it to me to-night, and usher in my happier years with music."

There was no denial to a request like that, and with a keen sense of delight Paul obeyed, singing as he had never sung before, for heart and soul were in the act, and all benignant influences lent their aid to beautify his gift. The silence of the night received the melody, and sent it whispering back like ripples breaking on the shore; the moonbeams danced like elves upon the keys, as if endowing human touch with their magnetic power; the west wind tuned its leafy orchestra to an airy symphony, and every odorous shrub and flower paid tribute to the happy hour.

With drooping lids and lips apart, Claudia listened, till on the surges of sweet sound her spirit floated far away into that blissful realm where human aspirations are fulfilled, where human hearts find their ideals, and renew again the innocent beliefs that made their childhood green.

Silence fell suddenly, startling Claudia from her dream. For a moment the radiance of the room grew dark before her eyes, then a swift light dawned, and in it she beheld the countenance of her friend transfigured by the power of that great passion which heaven has gifted with eternal youth. For a long moment nothing stirred, and across the little space that parted them the two regarded one another with wordless lips, but eyes whose finer language made all speech impertinent.

Paul bent on the woman whom he loved a look more tender than the most impassioned prayer, more potent than the subtlest appeal, more eloquent than the most fervent vow. He saw the maiden color flush and fade, saw the breath quicken and the lips grow tremulous, but the steadfast eyes never wavered, never fell, and through those windows of the soul, her woman's heart looked out and answered him.

There was no longer any doubt or fear or power to part them now, and with a gesture full of something nobler than Pride, Paul stretched his hand to Claudia, and she took it fast in both her own.

To a believer in metempsychosis it would have been an easy task to decide the last shape Mrs. Snowden had endowed with life, for the old fable of the "cat transformed into a woman," might have been again suggested to a modern Aesop.

Soft of manner, smooth of tongue, stealthy of eye, this feline lady followed out the instincts of her nature with the fidelity of any veritable puss. With demure aspect and pleasant purrings she secured the admiration of innocents who forgot that velvet paws could scratch, and the friendship of comfortable souls who love to pet and be amused. Daintily picking her way through the troubles of this life, she slipped into cosy corners where rugs were softest and fires warmest, gambolling delightfully while the cream was plentiful, and the caresses graciously bestowed. Gossips and scandal were the rats and mice she feasted on, the prey she paraded with ill-disguised exultation when her prowlings and pouncings had brought them to light. Many a smart robin had been fascinated by her power, or escaping left his plumes behind; many a meek mouse had implored mercy for its indiscretion but found none, and many a blithe cricket's music ended when she glided through the grass. Dark holes and corners were hunted by her keen eye, the dust of forgotten rumors was disturbed by her covert tread, and secrets were hunted out with most untiring patience.

She had her enemies, what puss has not? Sundry honest mastiffs growled when she entered their domains, but scorned to molest a weaker foe; sundry pugs barked valiantly till she turned on them and with unsheathed claws administered a swift quietus to their wrath; sundry jovial squirrels cracked their jokes and flourished defiance, but skipped nimbly from her way, and chattered on a bow she could not climb. More than one friend had found the pantry pillaged, and the milk of human kindness lapped dry by an indefatigable tongue; and yet no meeker countenance lifted its pensive eyes in church, no voice more indignantly rebuked the shortcomings of her race, and no greater martyr bewailed ingratitude when doors were shut upon her, and stern housewives shouted "scat!"

Wifehood and widowhood had only increased her love of freedom and confirmed her love of power. Claudia pitied her, and when others blamed, defended or excused, for her generous nature had no knowledge of duplicity or littleness of soul. Jessie seemed all candor, and though superficial, was full of winning ways and tender confidences that seemed sincere, and very pleasant to the other's lonely heart. So Jessie haunted her friend's house, rode triumphantly in her carriage, made a shield of her regard, and disported herself at her expense, till a stronger force appeared, and the widow's reign abruptly ended.

The May moon had shown on Claudia's betrothal, and the harvest moon would shine upon her marriage. The months passed like a happy dream, and the midsummer of her life was in its prime. The stir and tattle that went on about her was like an idle wind, for she had gone out of the common world and believed that she cared little for its censure or its praise. What mattered it that Paul was poor—she was not rich? What mattered it that she knew little of his past—had she not all the present and the future for her own? What cared she for the tongues that called him "fortune-hunter", and herself romantic? he possessed a better fortune than any she could give, and she was blessed with a romance that taught her wiser lessons than reality had ever done. So they went their way, undisturbed by any wind that blew. Paul still gave her lessons, still retained his humble home as if no change had befallen him, and Claudia with all her energies alert, bestirred herself to "set her house in order, and make ready for the bridegroom's coming." But as each night fell, patient Teacher, busy Housewife vanished, and two lovers met. The sun set on all their cares, and twilight shed a peace upon them softer than the dew, for Joy was the musician now, and Love the fairy hostess of the guests who made high festival of that still hour.

The months had dwindled to a week, and in the gloaming of a sultry day, Paul came early to his tryst. Claudia was detained by lingering guests, and with a frown at their delay, her lover paced the room until she should come. Pausing suddenly in his restless march, Paul drew a letter from his breast and read it slowly as if his thoughts had been busy with its contents. It was a letter of many pages, written in decided characters, worn as if with frequent reading, and as he turned it his face wore a look it had never shown to Claudia's eyes. With a sudden impulse he raised his right hand to the light, and scanned it with a strange scrutiny. Across the palm stretched a wide purple scar, the relic of some wound healed long ago, but not effaced by time. Claudia had once asked as she caressed it what blow had left so deep a trace, and he had answered with a sudden clenching of the hand, a sudden fire in the eye, "Claudia, it is the memorial of a victory I won ten years ago; it was a righteous battle, but its memory is bitter. Let it sleep; and believe me, it is an honest hand, or I could never look in your true face and give it you again."

She had been content, and never touched the sad past by a word, for she wholly trusted where she wholly loved.

As Paul looked thoughtfully at that right hand of his, the left dropped at his side, and from among the loosely held papers, a single sheet escaped, and fluttered noiselessly among the white folds of the draperies, that swept the floor. The stir of departing feet aroused him from his reverie; with a quick gesture he crushed the letter, and lit it at the Roman lamp that always burned for him. Slowly the fateful pages shrivelled and grew black; silently he watched them burn, and when the last flame flickered and went out, he gathered up the ashes and gave them to the keeping of the wind. Then all the shadows faded from his face, and left the old composure there.

Claudia's voice called from below, and with the ardor of a boy he sprang down to meet the welcome he was hungering for.

As the door closed behind him, from the gloom of that inner room Jessie Snowden stole out and seized her prize. Listening with sharpened sense for any coming step, she swept the page with her keen eye, gathering its meaning before a dozen lines were read. The paper rustled with the tremor of her hand, and for a moment the room spun dizzily before her as she dropped into a seat, and sat staring straight into the air with a countenance where exultation and bewilderment were strangely blended. "Poor Claudia," was the first thought that took shape in her mind, but a harder one usurped its place, an ominous glitter shone in her black eyes, as she muttered with a wicked smile, "I owe him this, and he shall have it."

An hour later Paul and Claudia sat in that same spot together, not yet content, for opposite still lounged Jessie Snowden, showing no symptoms of departure. Her cheek burned with a brilliant color, her black eyes glittered with repressed excitement and in gesture, look and tone there was a peculiar sharpness as if every sense were unwontedly alert, every nerve unwontedly high strung. She was not loquacious, but seemed waiting till speech would take effect; for all her feline instincts were awake, and she must torture a little before she dealt the blow. She knew the lovers wished her gone, yet still sat watchful and wary, till the auspicious moment came.

Paul was restless, for his southern temperament, more keenly alive to subtle influences than colder natures, vaguely warned him of the coming blow, unwillingly yielded to the baleful power it could not comprehend, unconsciously betrayed that Jessie's presence brought disquiet, and so doing placed a weapon in her hand, which she did not fail to use. Her eye was on him constantly, with a glance that stirred him like an insult, while it held him like a spell. His courtesy was sorely tried, for whether he spoke or was mute, moved about the room or sat with averted face, he felt that eye still on him, with a look of mingled hatred, pity and contempt. He confronted it and bore it down; but when he turned, it rose again and haunted him with its aggressive shine. He fixed his regard on Claudia, and so forgot for a time, but it was always there and proved itself no fancy of a tired brain.

Claudia was weary and grudged the quiet hour which always left her refreshed, when no unwelcome presence marred its charm. She was unutterably tired of Jessie, and if a wish could have secured her absence, she would have vanished with the speed of a stage sprite at the wizard's will.

"Is't the old pain, Paul? Let me play Desdemona, and bind my handkerchief about your forehead as I have done before," and Claudia's voice soothed the ear with unspoken love.

Paul had leaned his head upon his hand, but as she spoke he lifted it and answered cheerfully, "I have no pain, but something in the atmosphere oppresses me. I fancy there is thunder in the air."

"There is"—and Jessie laughed a laugh that had no mirth in it, as she sat erect with sudden interest in her voice.

Paul swept aside the curtain, and looked out; the sky was cloudless and the evening star hung luminous and large on the horizon's edge.

"Ah, you think I am a false prophet, but wait an hour then look again. *I* see a fierce storm rolling up, though the cloud is 'no bigger than a man's hand' now."

As she spoke Jessie's eye glanced across the hand Paul had extended for the fan which Claudia was offering; he did not see the look, but unfurling the daintily carved toy, answered calmly as the stirred air cooled the fever of his cheek: "I cannot doubt you, Mrs. Snowden, for you look truly sibylline tonight; but if you read the future with such a gifted eye, can you not find us a fairer future than your storm foretells?"

"Did you ever know before that there was gipsy blood in my veins, and that I possessed the gipsy's power of second sight? Shall I use it, and tell your fortune like a veritable witch? May I, Claudia?"

Jessie's friend looked at her with a touch of wonder; for the flush was deepening on her cheek, the fire kindling in her eyes, and her whole aspect seemed to stir and brighten like a snake's before it springs.

"If Paul pleases I should like to hear your 'rede,' and we will cross your palm with silver by and by. Indeed I think the inspired phrenzy is descending upon you, Jessie, for you look like an electric battery fully charged, and I dare not touch you lest I should receive a shock," Claudia answered, smiling at the sudden change.

"I *am* a battery to-night, and you *may* have your shock whenever you please. Come, Mr. Frere, your sovereign consents, come and let me try my power—if you dare."

A slight frown contracted Paul's brows, and a disdainful smile flitted across his lips; but Claudia waited and he silently obeyed.

"Not this hand, fate lies only in the *right*."

"Jessie, take mine instead, our fortunes henceforth will be the same!" cried Claudia, with eager voice remembering the mark Paul never showed.

But Jessie only laughed the metallic laugh again, clear and sharp as the jangle of a bell; and with a gesture of something like defiance Paul stretched his right hand to her, while the disdainful smile still sat upon his lips. Jessie did not touch it, but bent and scanned it eagerly, though nothing could be seen but the wide scar across the shapely palm.

A dead silence fell upon the three. Paul stood composed and motionless, Jessie paled visibly, and the quick throb of her heart grew audible, but Claudia felt the pain of that rude scrutiny, and leaning toward them asked impatiently, "Sibyl, what do you read?"

Jessie swayed slowly backward, and looking up at the defiant face above her, answered in a whisper that cut the silence like a knife.

"I see two letters,—M. L."

Paul did not start, his countenance did not change, but the fan dropped shattered from his grasp—the only sign that he had heard. Claudia's eyes were on them, but she could not speak, and the sibilant whisper came again.

"I know it all, for *this* remained to tell the secret, and *I* am the master now. See here!" and with a peal of laughter Jessie threw the paper at his feet.

CHAPTER IV

Paul gave one glance at the crumpled sheet, then turned on her with a look that sent her trembling to the door, as a gust would sweep a thistle down before it. It was the look of a hunted creature, driven to bay; wrath, abhorrence, and despair stirred the strong man's frame, looked out at his desperate eye, strengthened his uplifted arm, and had not his opponent been a woman some swift retribution would have fallen on her, for there was murder in his fiery blood.

Claudia sprang to his side, and at the touch of those restraining hands a stern pallor settled on his countenance, a hard-won self-control quenched his passion, a bitter truth confronted his despair, and left him desolate but not degraded. His eye fixed on Jessie, and its hopelessness was more eloquent than a torrent of entreaties, its contempt more keen than the sharpest reproach.

"Go," he said with a strange hush in his voice, "I ask nothing of you, for I know you would be merciless to me; but if there be any compassion, any touch of nobleness in your nature you will spare your friend, remembering what she has been to you. Go, and mar my hard-won reputation as you will, the world's condemnation I will not accept, my judge is *here.*"

"There will be no need of silence a week hence when the marriage day comes around and there is no bridegroom for the bride. I foretold the storm, and it has come; heaven help you through it, Claudia. Good night, pleasant dreams, and a fair tomorrow!"

Jessie Snowden tried to look exultant, but her white lips would not smile, and though the victory was hers she crept away like one who has suffered defeat.

Paul locked the door behind her, and turning, looked at Claudia with a world of anguish in his altered face. She moved as if to go to him, but a gesture arrested her, and uttering a broken exclamation Paul struck his scarred hand on the chimney piece with a force that left it bruised and bleeding, and dropping his hot forehead on the marble stood silent, struggling with a grief that had no solace.

Claudia paused a moment, mute and pale, watching the bowed figure and the red drops as they fell, then she went to him, and holding the wounded palm as if it were a suffering child, she laid her cheek to his, whispering tenderly: "Paul, you said this was an honest hand and I believe it still. There should not be a grain of dust between us two,—deal frankly with me now, and let me comfort you."

Paul lifted up his face wan with the tearless sorrow of a man, and gathering the beloved comforter close to his sore heart looked long into the countenance whose loving confidence had no reproach for him as yet. He held her fast for a little space, kissed her lips and forehead lingeringly, as if he took a mute farewell, then gently put her from him saying, as she sank into a seat—

"Claudia, I never meant to burden you with my unhappy past, believing that I did no wrong in burying it deep from human sight, and walking through the world as if it had never been. I see my error now, and bitterly I repent it. Put pity, prejudice, and pride away, and see me as I am. Hear and judge me, and by your judgment I will abide."

_M. L._

He paused, silently gathering calmness from his strength, and courage from his love; then, as if each word were wrung from him by a sharper pang than he had ever known before, he said slowly: "Claudia, those letters were once branded on my hand, they are the initials of a name— 'Maurice Lecroix.' Ten years ago he was my master, I his slave."

If Paul had raised his strong right arm and struck her, the act would not have daunted her with such a pale dismay, or shocked the power more rudely from her limbs. For an instant the tall shape wavered mistily before her and her heart stood still; then she girded up her energies, for with her own suffering came the memory of his, and, true woman through it all, she only covered up her face and cried: "Go on, I can hear it, Paul!"

Solemnly and steadily, as if it were his dying shrift, Paul stood before the woman he loved and told the story of his life.

"My father—God forgive him—was a Cuban planter, my mother a beautiful Quadroon, mercifully taken early out of slavery to an eternal freedom. I never knew her but she bequeathed to me my father's love, and I possessed it till he died. For fifteen years I was a happy child, and forgot that I was a slave—light tasks, kind treatment, and slight restraints so blinded me to the real hardships of my lot. I had a sister, heiress of my father's name and fortune, and she was my playmate all those years, sharing her pleasures and her pains with me, her small store of knowledge, her girlish accomplishments as she acquired them, and—more than all—the blessing of an artless love. I was her proud protector, her willing servitor, and in those childish days we were what heaven made us, brother and sister fond and free.

I was fifteen when my father died, and the black blight fell upon me in a single night. He had often promised me my freedom—strange gift from a father to a son!—but like other duties it had been neglected till too late. Death came suddenly, and I was left a sadder orphan than poor Nathalie, for my heritage was a curse that cancelled all past love by robbing me of liberty.

"Nathalie and I were separated—she went to her guardian's protection, I to the auction block. Her last words were, 'Be kind to Paul.' They promised; but when she was gone they sold me far away from my old home, and then I learned what it was to be a slave. Ah, Claudia, you shudder when I say those words; give your abhorrence to the man who dared to love you, but bestow a little pity on the desolate boy you never knew. I had a hard master, he a rebellious spirit to subdue; for I could not learn subjection, and my young blood burned within me at an insult or a blow. My father's kindness proved the direst misfortune that could have befallen me, for I had been lifted up into humanity and now I was cast back among the brutes; I had been born with a high heart and an eager spirit, they had been cherished fifteen years, now they were to be crushed and broken by inevitable fate.

"Year after year I struggled on, growing more desperate, and tugging more fiercely at my chain as each went by, bringing manhood but not the right to enjoy or make it mine. I tried to escape, but in vain, and each failure added to my despair. I tried to hear of Nathalie, but she had learned to look on me in another light, and had forgotten the sweet tie that bound us once. I tried to become a chattel and be content, but my father had given me his own free instincts, aspirations, and desires, and I could not change my nature though I were to be a slave forever.

"Five miserable years dragged by—so short to tell of, such an eternity to live! I was twenty, and no young man ever looked into the world more eager to be up and doing, no young man ever saw so black a future as that which appalled me with its doom. I would not accept it, but made a last resolve to try once more for liberty, and if I failed, to end the life I could no longer bear. Watchfully I waited, warily I planned, desperately I staked my last hope—and lost it. I was betrayed and hunted down as ruthlessly as any wolf; but I tried to keep my vow; for as my pursuers clutched me I struck the blow that should have ended all, and the happiest moment of my life was that swift pang when the world passed from me with the exultant thought, 'I am free at last!'"

Paul paused, spent and breathless with rapid speech and strong emotion, and in the silence heard Claudia murmuring through a rain of tears: "Oh, my love! my love! was there no friend but death?"

That low cry was a stronger cordial to Paul's spirit than the rarest wine grape that ever grew. He looked yearningly across the narrow space that parted them, but though his eye blessed her for her pity, he did not pass the invisible barrier he had set up between them till her hand should throw it down or fix it there forever.

"These are bitter things for you to hear, dear heart. God knows they were bitter things to bear, but I am stronger for them now and you the calmer for your tears. A little more and happier times are coming. I could not lie, but came out of that 'valley of the shadow' a meeker soul; for though branded, buffeted, and bruised, I clung to life, blindly believing help must come, and it did. One day a shape passed before my eyes that seemed the angel of deliverance—it was Nathalie, and she was my master's guest. I gathered covertly that she was a gentle-woman, that she was mistress of her fortune now, and soon to be a happy wife; and hearing these things I determined to make one appeal to her in my great need.

"I watched her, and one blessed night, defying every penalty, and waiting till the house was still, and her light burned alone as I had seen it many times before, I climbed the balcony and stood before her saying, 'I am Paul, help me in our father's name.' She did not recognize the blithe boy in the desperate man, but I told my misery, implored compassion and relief, I looked at her with her father's face, and nature pleaded better than my prayers, for she stretched her hands to me, saying, with tears as beautiful as those now shining on your cheek, 'Who should help you if not I? Be comforted and I will atone for this great neglect and wrong. Paul, have faith in me; I shall not fail.'

"Claudia, you loved me first for my great reverence for woman-kind; this is the secret of the virtue you commend, for when I was most desolate a woman succored me. Since then, in every little maid, I see the child who loved me when a boy, in every blooming girl, the Nathalie who saved me when a man, in every woman, high or low, the semblance of my truest friend, and do them honor in my sister's name."

"Heaven crown her with a happy life!" prayed Claudia, with fervent heart, and still more steadily her lover's voice went on.

"She kept her word, and did a just deed generously, for money flowed like water till I was free, then giving me a little store for present needs, she sent me out the richest man that walked the world. I left the island and went to and fro seeking for my place upon the earth. I never told my story, never betrayed my past, I have no sign of my despised race but my Spanish hue, and taking my father's native country for my own I found no bar in swarthy skin, or the only name I had a right to bear. I seared away all traces of a master's claim, and smiled as the flame tortured me, for liberty had set her seal upon my forehead, and my flesh and blood were *mine.*

"Then I took the rights and duties of a man upon me, feeling their weight and worth, looking proudly on them as a sacred trust won by much suffering, to be used worthily and restored to their bestower richer for my stewardship. I looked about me for some work to do, for now I labored for myself, and industry was sweet. I was a stranger in a strange land, friendless and poor; but I had energy and hope, two angels walking with me night and day.

"Music had always been my passion; now I chose it as my staff of life. In hospitable Germany I made true friends who aided me, and doing any honest work by day, I gave my nights to study, trying to repair the loss of years.

"Southern trees grow rapidly, for their sap is stirred by whirlwinds and fed with ardent heats. Fast I struggled up, groping for the light that dawned more fairly as I climbed; and when ten years were gone I seemed to have been born anew. Paul the slave was dead and his grave grown green; Paul the man had no part in him beyond the mournful memory of the youth that pined and died too soon. The world had done me a great wrong, yet I asked no atonement but the liberty to prove myself a man; no favor but the right to bury my dead past and make my future what I would. Other men's ambitions were not mine, for twenty years had been taken from me and I had no time to fight for any but the highest prize. I was grateful for the boon heaven sent me, and felt that my work was to build up an honest life, to till the nature given me, and sow therein a late harvest, that my sheaf might yet be worthy the Great Reaper's hand. If there be any power in sincere desire, any solace in devout belief,—that strength, that consolation will be mine. Man's opprobrium may oppress me, woman's pity may desert me, suffering and wrong may still pursue me,—yet I am not desolate; for when all human charities have cast me off I know that a Diviner love will take me in."

To Paul's voice came the music of a fervent faith, in his eye burned the fire of a quenchless hope, and on his countenance there shone a pale serenity that touched it with the youth time cannot take away. Past and present faded from his sight, for in that moment his spirit claimed its birthright, and beyond the creature of his love, his heart beheld the aspiration of his life.

"Claudia, I never thought to know affection like your own; never thought I could deserve so great a blessing; but when it came to me in tenderest guise, pleading to be taken in, how could I bar the door to such a welcome visitant? I did not, and the strong sweet angel entered in to kindle on my lonely hearth a household fire that can never die. Heaven help me if the ministering spirit goes!"

Through all the story of his own despairs and griefs Paul had not faltered, but gone resolutely on, painting his sufferings lightly for Claudia's sake, but now when he remembered the affection she had cherished, the anguish she might feel, the confidence she might believe betrayed, a keen remorse assailed him, and his courage failed. He thought of Claudia lost, and with an exclamation of passionate regret paced the long room with restless feet—paused for a little, looking out into the magic stillness of the night, and came back calm again.

"When you first gave me the good gift you have a right to take again, I told you I was orphaned, friendless, poor; but I did not tell you why I was thus desolate, believing it was wiser to leave a bitter history untold. I thought I did no wrong, but I have learned that perfect peace is only found in perfect truth; and I accept the lesson, for I was too proud of my success, and I am cast down into the dust to climb again with steadier feet. I let you judge me as an equal, showing you my weaknesses, my wants, my passions, and beliefs, as any happier lover might have done; you found some spark of manhood there, for you loved me, and that act should have made me worthier of the gift—but it did not. Claudia, forgive me; I was weak, but I struggled to be strong; for in the blissful months that have gone by, you showed me all your heart, enriched me with your confidence, and left no sorrow of your life untold—this brave sincerity became a mute reproach to me at last, for far down in *my* heart was a secret chamber never opened to your eye, for there my lost youth lay so stark and cold I dared not show you its dead face. But as the time came nearer when you were to endow me with the name which should go hand in hand with innocence and truth, this vague remorse for a silent wrong determined me to make confession of my past. I wrote it all, believing I could never tell it, as I have done to-night, learning that love can cast out fear. I wrote it and brought it many times, but never gave it, for O, Claudia! O, my heart! I loved you more than honor, and I could not give you up!"

From sleeping garden and still night a breath of air sighed through the room, as mournful and as sweet as those impassioned words, but Claudia never lifted up her hidden face, or stirred to answer it, for she was listening to a more divine appeal, and taking counsel in the silence of her heart.

Paul watched her, and the shadow of a great fear fell upon his face.

"I brought this confession here to-night, resolved to give it and be satisfied; but you did not come to meet me, and while I waited my love tempted me; the strong moment passed, and I burned it, yielding the nobler purpose for the dearer peace. This single page, how dropped I cannot tell, betrayed me to that—woman, and her malice forced on me the part I was not brave enough to play alone.

"Now, Claudia, all is told. Now, seeing what I have been, knowing what I desired to be, remembering mercifully what I am, try my crime and adjudge my punishment."

There was no need of that appeal, for judgment had been given long before the prayer came. Pride, and fear, and shame had dropped away, leaving the purer passion free; now justice and mercy took love by the hand and led it home. On Claudia's face there came a light more beautiful than any smile; on cheek and forehead glowed the fervor of her generous blood, in eye and voice spoke the courage of her steadfast heart, as she flung down the barrier, saying only: "Mine still, mine forever, Paul!" and with that tender welcome took the wronged man to the shelter of her love.

Tears hot and heavy as a summer rain baptised the new born peace and words of broken gratitude sang its lullaby, as that strong nature cradled it with blessings and with prayers. Paul was the weaker now, and Claudia learned the greatness of past fear by the vehemence of present joy, as they stood together tasting the sweetness of a moment that enriched their lives.

"Love, do you remember what this gift may cost? Do you remember what I am henceforth to other eyes? Can you bear to see familiar faces growing strange to you, to meet looks that wound you with their pity, to hear words that sting you with their truth, and find a shadow falling on your life from me?"

As he spoke, Paul lifted up that face, "clear-shining after rain," but it did not alter, did not lose its full content, as Claudia replied with fervent voice: "I do remember that I cannot pay too much for what is priceless; that when I was loveless and alone, there came a friend who never will desert me when all others fail; that from lowly places poets, philosophers, and kings have come; and when the world sneers at the name you give me, I can turn upon it saying with the pride that stirs me now: 'My husband has achieved a nobler success than men you honor, has surmounted greater obstacles, has conquered sterner foes, and risen to be an honest man.' "

Paul proved that he was one by still arming her against himself, still warning her of the cruel prejudices which he had such sad cause to know and fear.

"Your generous nature blinds you to the trials I foresee, the disappointments I foretell. In your world there will be no place for me, when this is known, and I cannot ask you to come down from your high place to sit beside an outcast's fire. I have not lost your love,—that was the blow I feared; and still possessing it I can relinquish much, and yield the new title I was soon to know, if I may keep the dear old one of 'friend.' It is no longer in our power to keep this secret unknown, and strengthen our affection by it, as I once hoped. Think of this, Claudia, in a calmer mood, weigh well the present and the future cost, for you have the power to make or mar your happiness.

"No loss of yours must be my gain, and I had rather never look into this face again than live to see it saddened by a vain regret for any act I might have saved you from by timely pain."

"I will consider, I will prove myself before I take your peace into my hands; but, Paul, I know the answer that will come to all my doubts, I know I shall not change."

Claudia spoke steadily, for she knew herself; and when at length her lover went, her last words were, "Believe in me, I shall not change."

Slowly the clear flame of the lamp grew dim and died, softly Night sang her cradle hymn to hush the weary world, and solemnly the silence deepened as the hours went by, but Claudia with wakeful eyes trod to and fro, or sat an image of mute thought. She was not alone, for good and evil spirits compassed her about, making that still room the battle-field of a viewless conflict between man's law, and woman's love. All the worldly wisdom time had taught, now warned her of the worldly losses she might yet sustain, all the prejudices born of her position and strengthened by her education now assailed her with covert skill, all the pride grown with her growth now tempted her to forget the lover in the slave, and fear threatened her with public opinion, that grim ghost that haunts the wisest and the best. But high above the voice of pride, the sigh of fear, and the echo of "the world's dread laugh," still rose the whisper of her heart, undaunted, undismayed, and cried to her,—

"I was cold, and he cherished me beside his fire; hungry, and he gave me food; a stranger, and he took me in."

Slowly the moon climbed the zenith and dropped into the West, slowly the stars paled one by one, and the gray sky kindled ruddily as dawn came smiling from the hills. Slowly the pale shadow of all worldliness passed from Claudia's mind, and left it ready for the sun, slowly the spectral doubts, regrets and fears vanished one by one, and through the twilight of that brief eclipse arose the morning of a fairer day.

As young knights watched their arms of old in chapels haunted by the memory of warrior or saint, and came forth eager for heroic deeds, so Claudia in the early dawn braced on the armor consecrated by a night of prayerful vigil, and with valiant soul addressed herself to the duty which would bring her life's defeat or victory.

Paul found another Claudia than the one he left; for a woman steadfast and strong turned to him a countenance as full of courage as of cheer, when standing there again he looked deep into her eyes and offered her his hand as he had done on that betrothal night. Now, as then, she took it, and in a moment gave a sweet significance to those characters which were the only vestiges of his wrong, for bending she touched the scarred palm with her lips, and whispered tenderly, "My love, there is no anguish in that brand, no humiliation in that claim, and I accept the bondage of the master who rules all the world."

As he spoke, Paul looked a happier, more *contented* slave, than those fabulous captives the South boasts of, but finds it hard to show.

Claudia led him back into the lower world again by asking with a sigh— "Paul, why should Jessie Snowden wish to wound me so? What cause have I given her for such dislike?"

A swift color swept across her lover's face, and the disdainful smile touched his lips again as he replied, "It is not a thing for me to tell; yet for the truth's sake I must. Jessie Snowden wooed what Claudia won. Heaven knows I have no cause for vanity, yet I could not help seeing in her eyes the regard it took so long to read in these more maidenly ones. I had no return to make, but gave all the friendship and respect I could to one for whom I had a most invincible distaste. There was no other cause for her dislike, yet I believe she hated me, or why should she speak with such malicious pleasure where a more generous woman would have held her peace? I have no faith in her, and by tomorrow I shall see in some changed face the first cloud of the storm she once foretold. Claudia, let us be married quietly, and go away until the gossips are grown weary, and we are forgotten."

Paul spoke with the sudden impulse of a nature sensitive and proud, but Claudia's energy was fully aroused and she answered with indignant color, "No, nothing must be changed. I asked my friends to see me made a proud and happy wife; shall I let them think I am ashamed to stand before them with the man I love? Paul, if I cannot bear a few harsh words, a few cold looks, a little pain, for you, of what worth is my love, of what use is my strength, and how shall I prove a fit friend and help-meet to you in the heavier cares and sorrows heaven sends us all?"

"Claudia, you are the braver of the two! I should be stronger if I had much to give; but I am so poor, this weight of obligation robs me of my courage. I am a weak soul, love, for I cannot trust, and I am still haunted by the fear that I shall one day read some sorrowful regret in this face, grown so wan with one night's watching for my sake."

Claudia dropped on her knee before him, and lifting up her earnest countenance, said, "Read it, Paul, and never doubt again. You spoke once of atonement,—make it by conquering your pride and receiving as freely as I give; for believe me, it is as hard a thing greatly to accept, as it is bountifully to bestow. You are not poor, for there can be no mine and thine between us two; you are not weak, for I lean on your strength, and know it will not fail; you are not fearful now, for looking here, you see the wife who never can regret or know the shadow of a change." Paul brushed the brown locks back, and as he read it smiled again, for heart and eyes and tender lips confirmed the truth, and he was satisfied.

Jessie Snowden's secret haunted her like Lady Macbeth's, and like that strong-minded woman, she would have told it in her sleep, if she had not eased herself by confiding it to a single friend. "Dear Maria" promised an eternal silence, but "Dear Maria" was the well known "little bird" who gave the whisper to the air. Rumor sowed it broadcast, gossips nurtured it, and Claudia reaped a speedy harvest of discomforts and chagrins.

She thought herself well armed for the "war of words"; but women's tongues forged weapons whose blows she could not parry, and men's censure or coarse pity pierced her shield, and wounded deeper than she dared to tell. Her "dear five hundred friends" each came to save her from social suicide, and her peaceful drawing-room soon became a chamber of the Inquisition, where a daily "Council of Ten" tormented her with warnings, entreaties—and reproaches,—harder trials for a woman to bear, than the old tortures of rack and thirst and fire.

She bore herself bravely through these troublous times, but her pillow received bitter tears, heard passionate prayers and the throbbing of an indignant heart, that only calmed itself by the power of its love. Paul never saw a tear or heard a sigh,—for him the steady smile sat on her lips, a cheerful courage filled her eye; but he read her pain in the meekness which now beautified her face, and silently the trial now drew them nearer than before.

There was no mother to gather Claudia to her breast with blessings and with prayers when the marriage morning dawned, no sister to hover near her, April-like, with smiles and tears, no father to give her proudly to the man she loved, and few friends to make it a blithe festival; but a happier bride had never waited for her bridegroom's coming than Claudia as she looked out at the sunshine of a gracious day, and said within herself, "Heaven smiles upon me with auspicious skies, and in the depths of my own heart I hear a sweeter chime than any wedding bells can ring,—feel a truer peace than human commendation can bestow. Oh father, whom I never knew! oh mother, whom I wholly loved! be with me now, and bless me in this happy hour."

Paul came at last, fevered with the disquiet of much sleepless thought, and still disturbed by the gratitude of a generous nature, which believed itself unworthy of the gift relenting Fortune now bestowed. He saw a fair woman crowned for him, and remembering his past, looked at her, saying with troubled and agitated voice—"Claudia, it is not yet too late." But the white shape fluttered from him to the threshold of the door, and looking back, only answered, "Come."

Music, the benignant spirit of their lives, breathed a solemn welcome as the solitary pair paced down the chancel, through the silken stir of an uprising throng. Down from the altar window, full of sacred symbols and rich hues, fell heaven's benediction in a flood of light, touching Paul's bent head with mellow rays, and bathing Claudia's bridal snow in bloom.

Silently that unconscious pair preached a better sermon than had ever echoed there, for it appealed to principles that never die, and made its text, "The love of liberty, the liberty of love."

Many a worldly man forgot his worldliness, and thinking of Paul's hard-won success, owned that he honored him. Many a frivolous woman felt her eye wet by sudden dew, her bosom stirred by sudden sympathy, as Claudia's clear, "I will," rose through the hush, and many a softened heart confessed the beauty of the deed it had condemned.

Stern bridegroom and pale bride, those two had come into the chapel's gloom; proud-eyed husband, blooming wife, those two made one, passed out into the sunlight on the sward, and down along that shining path they walked serenely into their new life.

The nine days' wonder died away and Paul and Claudia, listening to the murmur of the sea, forgot there was a world through all that happy month. But when they came again and took their places in the circle they had left, the old charm had departed; for prejudice, a sterner autocrat than the Czar of all the Russias, hedged them round with an invisible restraint, that seemed to shut them out from the genial intercourse they had before enjoyed. Claudia would take no hand that was not given as freely to her husband, and there were not many to press her own as cordially as they once had done. Then she began to realize the emptiness of her old life, for now she looked upon it with a clearer eye, and saw it would not stand the test she had applied.

This was the lesson she had needed, it taught her the value of true friendship, showed her the poverty of old beliefs, the bitterness of old desires, and strengthened her proud nature by the sharp discipline of pain.

Paul saw the loneliness that sometimes came upon her when her former pleasures ceased to satisfy, and began to feel that his forebodings would prove true. But they never did; for there came to them those good Samaritans who minister to soul as well as sense; these took them by the hand,

and through their honor for her husband, gave to Claudia the crowning lesson of her life.

They led her out of the world of wealth, and fashion, and pretense, into that other world that lies above it, full of the beauty of great deeds, high thoughts and humble souls, who walk its ways, rich in the virtues that

> "Smell sweet, and blossom in the dust."

Like a child in fairyland she looked about her, feeling that here she might see again the aspirations of her youth, and find those happy visions true.

In this new world she found a finer rank than any she had left, for men whose righteous lives were their renown, whose virtues their estate, were peers of this realm, whose sovereign was Truth, whose ministers were Justice and Humanity, whose subjects all "who loved their neighbor better than themselves."

She found a truer chivalry than she had known before, for heroic deeds shone on her in the humblest guise, and she discovered knights of a nobler court than Arthur founded, or than Spenser sang. Saint Georges, valiant as of old, Sir Guyons, devout and strong, and silver-tongued Sir Launcelots without a stain, all fighting the good fight for love of God and universal right.

She found a fashion old as womanhood and beautiful as charity, whose votaries lived better poems than any pen could write; brave Britomarts redressing wrongs, meek Unas succoring the weak, high-hearted Maids of Orleans steadfast through long martyrdoms of labor for the poor, all going cheerfully along the by-ways of the world, and leaving them the greener for the touch of their unwearied feet.

She found a religion that welcomed all humanity to its broad church, and made its priest the peasant of Judea who preached the Sermon on the Mount.

Then, seeing these things, Claudia felt that she had found her place, and putting off her "purple of fine linen," gave herself to earnest work, which is the strengthening wine of life. Paul was no longer friendless and without a home, for here he found a country, and a welcome to that brotherhood which makes the whole world kin; and like the pilgrims in that fable never old, these two "went on their way rejoicing," leaving the shores of "Vanity Fair" behind them, and through the "Valley of Humiliation" climbed the mountains whence they saw the spires of the "Celestial City" shining in the sun.

Slowly all things right themselves when founded on truth. Time brought tardy honors to Paul, and Claudia's false friends beckoned her to come and take her place again, but she only touched the little heads, looked up into her husband's face, and answered with a smile of beautiful content—"I cannot give the substance for the shadow,—cannot leave my world for yours. Put off the old delusions that blind you to the light, and come up here to me."

NELLY'S HOSPITAL

*N*ELLY sat beside her mother picking lint; but while her fingers flew, her eyes often looked wistfully out into the meadow, golden with buttercups, and bright with sunshine. Presently she said, rather bashfully, but very earnestly, "Mamma, I want to tell you a little plan I've made, if you'll please not laugh."

"I think I can safely promise that, my dear," said her mother, putting down her work that she might listen quite respectfully.

Nelly looked pleased, and went on confidingly. "Since brother Will came home with his lame foot, and I've helped you tend him, I've heard a great deal about hospitals, and liked it very much. To-day I said I wanted to go and be a nurse, like Aunt Mercy; but Will laughed, and told me I'd better begin by nursing sick birds and butterflies and pussies before I tried to take care of men. I did not like to be made fun of, but I've been thinking that it would be very pleasant to have a little hospital all my own, and be a nurse in it, because, if I took pains, so many pretty creatures might be made well, perhaps. Could I, mamma?"

Her mother wanted to smile at the idea, but did not, for Nelly looked up with her heart and eyes so full of tender compassion, both for the unknown men for whom her little hands had done their best, and for the smaller sufferers nearer home, that she stroked the shining head, and answered readily: "Yes, Nelly, it will be a proper charity for such a young Samaritan, and you may learn much if you are in earnest. You must study how to feed and nurse your little patients, else your pity will do no good, and your hospital become a prison. I will help you, and Tony shall be your surgeon."

"O mamma, how good you always are to me! Indeed, I am truly in earnest; I will learn, I will be kind, and may I go now and begin?"

"You may, but tell me first where will you have your hospital?"

First published in *Our Young Folks* (Boston: Ticknor and Fields, 1863). Reprinted in *Aunt Jo's Scrap Bag, Cupid and Chow-Chow*, vol. 3, 1874.

"In my room, mamma; it is so snug and sunny, and I never should forget it there," said Nelly.

"You must not forget it anywhere. I think that plan will not do. How would you like to find caterpillars walking in your bed, to hear sick pussies mewing in the night, to have beetles clinging to your clothes, or see mice, bugs, and birds tumbling down stairs whenever the door was open?" said her mother.

Nelly laughed at that thought a minute, then clapped her hands, and cried: "Let us have the old summer-house! My doves only use the upper part, and it would be so like Frank in the story-book. Please say yes again, mamma."

Her mother did say yes, and snatching up her hat, Nelly ran to find Tony, the gardener's son, a pleasant lad of twelve, who was Nelly's favorite playmate. Tony pronounced the plan a "jolly" one, and, leaving his work, followed his young mistress to the summer-house, for she could not wait one minute.

"What must we do first?" she asked, as they stood looking in at the dim, dusty room, full of garden tools, bags of seeds, old flower-pots, and watering-cans.

"Clear out the rubbish, miss," answered Tony.

"Here it goes, then," and Nelly began bundling everything out in such haste that she broke two flower-pots, scattered all the squash seeds, and brought a pile of rakes and hoes clattering down about her ears.

"Just wait a bit, and let me take the lead, miss. You hand me things, I'll pile 'em in the barrow and wheel 'em off to the barn; then it will save time, and be finished up tidy."

Nelly did as he advised, and very soon nothing but dust remained.

"What next?" she asked, not knowing in the least.

"I'll sweep up while you see if Polly can come and scrub the room out. It ought to be done before you stay here, let alone the patients."

"So it had," said Nelly, looking very wise all of a sudden. "Will says the wards—that means the rooms, Tony—are scrubbed every day or two, and kept very clean, and well venti—something—I can't say it; but it means having a plenty of air come in. I can clean windows while Polly mops, and then we shall soon be done."

Away she ran, feeling very busy and important. Polly came, and very soon the room looked like another place. The four latticed windows were set wide open, so the sunshine came dancing through the vines that grew outside, and curious roses peeped in to see what frolic was afoot. The walls shone white again, for not a spider dared to stay; the wide seat which encircled the room was dustless now,—the floor as nice as willing hands could make it; and the south wind blew away all musty odors with its fragrant breath.

"How fine it looks!" cried Nelly, dancing on the doorstep, lest a footprint should mar the still damp floor.

"I'd almost like to fall sick for the sake of staying here," said Tony, admiringly. "Now, what sort of beds are you going to have, miss?"

"I suppose it won't do to put butterflies and toads and worms into beds like the real soldiers where Will was?" answered Nelly, looking anxious.

Tony could hardly help shouting at the idea; but, rather than trouble his little mistress, he said very soberly: "I'm afraid they wouldn't lay easy, not being used to it. Tucking up a butterfly would about kill him; the worms would be apt to get lost among the bed-clothes; and the toads would tumble out the first thing."

"I shall have to ask mamma about it. What will you do while I'm gone?" said Nelly, unwilling that a moment should be lost.

"I'll make frames for nettings to the window, else the doves will come in and eat up the sick people."

"I think they will know that it is a hospital, and be too kind to hurt or frighten their neighbors," began Nelly; but as she spoke, a plump white dove walked in, looked about with its red-ringed eyes, and quietly pecked up a tiny bug that had just ventured out from the crack where it had taken refuge when the deluge came.

"Yes, we must have the nettings. I'll ask mamma for some lace," said Nelly, when she saw that; and, taking her pet dove on her shoulder, told it about her hospital as she went toward the house; for, loving all little creatures as she did, it grieved her to have any harm befall even the least or plainest of them. She had a sweet child-fancy that her playmates understood her language as she did theirs, and that birds, flowers, animals, and insects felt for her the same affection which she felt for them. Love always makes friends, and nothing seemed to fear the gentle child; but welcomed her like a little sun who shone alike on all, and never suffered an eclipse.

She was gone some time, and when she came back her mind was full of new plans, one hand full of rushes, the other of books, while over her head floated the lace, and a bright green ribbon hung across her arm.

"Mamma says that the best beds will be little baskets, boxes, cages, and any sort of thing that suits the patient; for each will need different care and food and medicine. I have not baskets enough, so, as I cannot have pretty white beds, I am going to braid pretty green nests for my patients, and, while I do it, mamma thought you'd read to me the pages she has marked, so that we may begin right."

"Yes, miss; I like that. But what is the ribbon for?" asked Tony.

"O, that's for you. Will says that, if you are to be an army surgeon, you must have a green band on your arm; so I got this to tie on when we play hospital."

Tony let her decorate the sleeve of his gray jacket, and when the nettings were done, the welcome books were opened and enjoyed. It was a happy time, sitting in the sunshine, with leaves pleasantly astir all about them, doves cooing overhead, and flowers sweetly gossiping together through the summer afternoon. Nelly wove her smooth, green rushes, Tony pored over his pages, and both found something better than fairy legends in the family histories of insects, birds, and beasts. All manner of wonders appeared, and were explained to them, till Nelly felt as if a new world had been given her, so full of beauty, interest, and pleasure that she never could be tired of studying it. Many of these things were not strange to Tony, because, born among plants, he had grown up with them as if they were brothers and sisters, and the sturdy, brown-faced boy had learned many lessons which no poet or philosopher could have taught him, unless he had become as childlike as himself, and studied from the same great book.

When the baskets were done, the marked pages all read, and the sun began to draw his rosy curtains round him before smiling "Good night," Nelly ranged the green beds round the room, Tony put in the screens, and the hospital was ready. The little nurse was so excited that she could hardly eat her supper, and directly afterwards ran up to tell Will how well she had succeeded with the first part of her enterprise. Now brother Will was a brave young officer, who had fought stoutly and done his duty like a man. But when lying weak and wounded at home, the cheerful courage which had led him safely through many dangers seemed to have deserted him, and he was often gloomy, sad, or fretful, because he longed to be at his post again, and time passed very slowly. This troubled his mother, and made Nelly wonder why he found lying in a pleasant room so much harder than fighting battles or making weary marches. Anything that interested and amused him was very welcome, and when Nelly, climbing on the arm of his sofa, told her plans, mishaps, and successes, he laughed out more heartily than he had done for many a day, and his thin face began to twinkle with fun as it used to do so long ago. That pleased Nelly, and she chatted like any affectionate little magpie, till Will was really interested; for when one is ill, small things amuse.

"Do you expect your patients to come to you, Nelly?" he asked.

"No, I shall go and look for them. I often see poor things suffering in the garden, and the wood, and always feel as if they ought to be taken care of, as people are."

"You won't like to carry insane bugs, lame toads, and convulsive kittens in your hands, and they would not stay on a stretcher if you had one. You should have an ambulance and be a branch of the Sanitary Commission," said Will.

Nelly had often heard the words, but did not quite understand what they meant. So Will told her of that great and never-failing charity, to which thousands owe their lives; and the child listened with lips apart, eyes often full, and so much love and admiration in her heart that she could find no words in which to tell it. When her brother paused, she said earnestly: "Yes, I will be a Sanitary. This little cart of mine shall be my amb'lance, and I'll never let my water-barrels go empty, never drive too fast, or be rough with my poor passengers, like some of the men you tell about. Does this look like an ambulance, Will?"

"Not a bit, but it shall, if you and mamma like to help me. I want four long bits of cane, a square of white cloth, some pieces of thin wood, and the gum-pot," said Will, sitting up to examine the little cart, feeling like a boy again as he took out his knife and began to whittle.

Up stairs and down stairs ran Nelly till all necessary materials were collected, and almost breathlessly she watched her brother arch the canes over the cart, cover them with the cloth, and fit in an upper shelf of small compartments, each lined with cotton-wool to serve as beds for wounded insects, lest they should hurt one another or jostle out. The lower part was left free for any larger creatures which Nelly might find. Among her toys she had a tiny cask which only needed a peg to be water-tight; this was filled and fitted in before, because, as the small sufferers needed no seats, there was no place for it behind, and, as Nelly was both horse and driver, it was more convenient in front. On each side of it stood a box of stores. In one were minute rollers, as bandages are called, a few bottles not yet filled, and a wee doll's jar of cold cream, because Nelly could not feel that her outfit was complete without a medicine chest. The other box was full of crumbs, bits of sugar, bird seed, and grains of wheat and corn, lest any famished stranger should die for want of food before she got it home. Then mamma painted "U. S. San. Com.," in bright letters on the cover, and Nelly received her charitable plaything with a long sigh of satisfaction.

"Nine o'clock already. Bless me, what a short evening this has been," exclaimed Will, as Nelly came to give him her good-night kiss.

"And such a happy one," she answered. "Thank you very, very much, dear Will. I only wish my little amb'lance was big enough for you to go in,—I'd so like to give you the first ride."

"Nothing I should like better, if it were possible, though I've a prejudice against ambulances in general. But as I cannot ride, I'll try and hop out to your hospital to-morrow, and see how you get on,"—which was a great deal for Captain Will to say, because he had been too listless to leave his sofa for several days.

That promise sent Nelly happily away to bed, only stopping to pop her head out of the window to see if it was likely to be a fair day to-morrow, and to tell Tony about the new plan as he passed below.

"Where shall you go to look for your first load of sick folks, miss?" he asked.

"All round the garden first, then through the grove, and home across the brook. Do you think I can find any patients so?" said Nelly.

"I know you will. Good night, miss," and Tony walked away with a merry look on his face, that Nelly would not have understood if she had seen it.

Up rose the sun bright and early, and up rose Nurse Nelly almost as early and as bright. Breakfast was taken in a great hurry, and before the dew was off the grass this branch of the Sanitary Commission was all astir. Papa, mamma, big brother and baby sister, men and maids, all looked out to see the funny little ambulance depart, and nowhere in all the summer fields was there a happier child than Nelly, as she went smiling down the garden path, where tall flowers kissed her as she passed and every blithe bird seemed singing a "Good speed!"

"How I wonder what I shall find first," she thought, looking sharply on all sides as she went. Crickets chirped, grasshoppers leaped, ants worked busily at their subterranean houses, spiders spun shining webs from twig to twig, bees were coming for their bags of gold, and butterflies had just begun their holiday. A large white one alighted on the top of the ambulance, walked over the inscription as if spelling it letter by letter, then floated away from flower to flower, like one carrying the good news far and wide.

"Now every one will know about the hospital and be glad to see me coming," thought Nelly. And indeed it seemed so, for just then a black-bird, sitting on the garden wall, burst out with a song full of musical joy, Nelly's kitten came running after to stare at the wagon and rub her soft side against it, a bright-eyed toad looked out from his cool bower among the lily leaves, and at that minute Nelly found her first patient. In one of the dewy cobwebs hanging from a shrub near by sat a fat black and yellow spider, watching a fly whose delicate wings were just caught in the net. The poor fly buzzed pitifully, and struggled so hard that the whole web shook; but the more he struggled, the more he tangled himself, and the fierce spider was preparing to descend that it might weave a shroud about its prey, when a little finger broke the threads and lifted the fly safely into the palm of a hand, where he lay faintly humming his thanks.

Nelly had heard much about contrabands, knew who they were, and was very much interested in them; so, when she freed the poor black fly, she played he was her contraband, and felt glad that her first patient was one that needed help so much. Carefully brushing away as much of the web as she could, she left small Pompey, as she named him, to free his own legs, lest her clumsy fingers should hurt him; then she laid him in one of the soft beds with a grain or two of sugar if he needed refreshment, and bade him rest and recover from his fright, remembering that he was at liberty to fly away whenever he liked, because she had no wish to make a slave of him.

Feeling very happy over this new friend, Nelly went on singing softly as she walked, and presently she found a pretty caterpillar dressed in brown fur, although the day was warm. He lay so still she thought him dead, till he rolled himself into a ball as she touched him.

"I think you are either faint from the heat of this thick coat of yours, or that you are going to make a cocoon of yourself, Mr. Fuzz," said Nelly. "Now I want to see you turn into a butterfly, so I shall take you, and if you get lively again I will let you go. I shall play that you have given out on a march, as the soldiers sometimes do, and been left behind for the Sanitary people to see to."

In went sulky Mr. Fuzz, and on trundled the ambulance till a golden green rose-beetle was discovered, lying on his back kicking as if in a fit.

"Dear me, what shall I do for him?" thought Nelly. "He acts as baby did when she was so ill, and mamma put her in a warm bath. I haven't got my little tub here, or any hot water, and I'm afraid the beetle would not like it if I had. Perhaps he has pain in his stomach; I'll turn him over, and pat his back, as nurse does baby's when she cries for pain like that."

She set the beetle on his legs, and did her best to comfort him; but he was evidently in great distress, for he could not walk, and instead of lifting his emerald overcoat, and spreading the wings that lay underneath, he turned over again, and kicked more violently than before. Not knowing what to do, Nelly put him into one of her soft nests for Tony to cure if possible. She found no more patients in the garden except a dead bee, which she wrapped in a leaf, and took home to bury. When she came to the grove, it was so green and cool she longed to sit and listen to the whisper of the pines, and watch the larch-tassels wave in the wind. But, recollecting her charitable errand, she went rustling along the pleasant path till she came to another patient, over which she stood considering several minutes before she could decide whether it was best to take it to her hospital, because it was a little gray snake, with a bruised tail. She knew it would not hurt her, yet she was afraid of it; she thought it pretty, yet could not like it; she pitied its pain, yet shrunk from helping it, for it had a fiery eye, and a quivering tongue, that looked as if longing to bite.

"He is a rebel, I wonder if I ought to be good to him," thought Nelly, watching the reptile writhe with pain. "Will said there were sick rebels in his hospital, and one was very kind to him. It says, too, in my little book, 'Love your enemies.' I think snakes are mine, but I guess I'll try and love him because God made him. Some boy will kill him if I leave him here, and then perhaps his mother will be very sad about it. Come, poor worm, I wish to help you, so be patient, and don't frighten me."

Then Nelly laid her little handkerchief on the ground, and with a stick gently lifted the wounded snake upon it, and, folding it together, laid it in the ambulance. She was thoughtful after that, and so busy puzzling her young head about the duty of loving those who hate us, and being kind to those who are disagreeable or unkind, that she went through the rest of the wood quite forgetful of her work. A soft "Queek, queek!" made her look up and listen. The sound came from the long meadow grass, and, bending it carefully back, she found a half-fledged bird, with one wing trailing on the ground, and its eyes dim with pain or hunger.

"You darling thing, did you fall out of your nest and hurt your wing?" cried Nelly, looking up into the single tree that stood near by. No nest was to be seen, no parent birds hovering overhead, and little Robin could only tell its troubles in that mournful "Queek, queek, queek!"

Nelly ran to get both her chests, and, sitting down beside the bird, tried to feed it. To her great joy it ate crumb after crumb as if it were half starved, and soon fluttered nearer with a confiding fearlessness that made her very proud. Soon baby Robin seemed quite comfortable, his eye brightened, he "queeked" no more, and but for the drooping wing would have been himself again. With one of her bandages Nelly bound both wings closely to his sides for fear he should hurt himself by trying to fly; and though he seemed amazed at her proceedings, he behaved very well, only staring at her, and ruffling up his few feathers in a funny way that made her laugh. Then she had to discover some way of accommodating her two larger patients so that neither should hurt nor alarm the other. A bright thought came to her after much pondering. Carefully lifting the handkerchief, she pinned the two ends to the roof of the cart, and there swung little Forked-tongue, while Rob lay easily below.

By this time Nelly began to wonder how it happened that she found so many more injured things than ever before. But it never entered her innocent head that Tony had searched the wood and meadow before she was up, and laid most of these creatures ready to her hands, that she might not be disappointed. She had not yet lost her faith in fairies, so she fancied they too belonged to her small sisterhood, and presently it did really seem impossible to doubt that the good folk had been at work.

Coming to the bridge that crossed the brook, she stopped a moment to watch the water ripple over the bright pebbles, the ferns bend down to drink, and the funny tadpoles frolic in quieter nooks, where the sun shone, and the dragon-flies swung among the rushes. When Nelly turned to go on, her blue eyes opened wide, and the handle of the ambulance dropped with a noise that caused a stout frog to skip into the water heels over head. Directly in the middle of the bridge was a pretty green tent, made of two tall burdock leaves. The stems were stuck into cracks between the boards, the tips were pinned together with a thorn, and one great buttercup nodded in the doorway like a sleepy sentinel. Nelly stared and smiled, listened, and looked about on every side. Nothing was seen but the quiet meadow and the shady grove, nothing was heard but the babble of the brook and the cheery music of the bobolinks.

"Yes," said Nelly softly to herself, "that is a fairy tent, and in it I may find a baby elf sick with whooping cough or scarlet fever. How splendid it would be! only I could never nurse such a dainty thing."

Stooping eagerly, she peeped over the buttercup's drowsy head, and saw what seemed a tiny cock of hay. She had no time to feel disappointed, for the haycock began to stir, and, looking nearer, she beheld two silvery gray mites, who wagged wee tails, and stretched themselves as if they had just waked up. Nelly knew that they were young field-mice, and rejoiced over them, feeling rather relieved that no fairy had appeared, though she still believed them to have had a hand in the matter.

"I shall call the mice my Babes in the Wood, because they are lost and covered up with leaves," said Nelly, as she laid them in her snuggest bed, where they nestled close together, and fell fast asleep again.

Being very anxious to get home, that she might tell her adventures, and show how great was the need of a Sanitary Commission in that region, Nelly marched proudly up the avenue, and, having displayed her load, hurried to the hospital, where another applicant was waiting for her. On the step of the door lay a large turtle, with one claw gone, and on his back was pasted a bit of paper, with his name,—"Commodore Waddle, U.S.N." Nelly knew this was a joke of Will's, but welcomed the ancient mariner and called Tony to help her get him in.

All that morning they were very busy settling the new-comers, for both people and books had to be consulted before they could decide what diet and treatment was best for each. The winged contraband had taken Nelly at her word, and flown away on the journey home. Little Rob was put in a large cage, where he could use his legs, yet not injure his lame wing. Forked-tongue lay under a wire cover, on sprigs of fennel, for the gardener said that snakes were fond of it. The Babes in the Wood were put to bed in one of the rush baskets, under a cotton-wool coverlet. Greenback, the beetle, found ease for his unknown aches in the warm heart of a rose, where he sunned himself all day. The Commodore was made happy in a tub of water, grass, and stones, and Mr. Fuzz was put in a well-ventilated glass box to decide whether he would be a cocoon or not.

Tony had not been idle while his mistress was away, and he showed her the hospital garden he had made close by, in which were cabbage, nettle, and mignonette plants for the butterflies, flowering herbs for the bees, chickweed and hemp for the birds, catnip for the pussies, and plenty of room left for whatever other patients might need. In the afternoon, while Nelly did her task at lint-picking, talking busily to Will as she worked, and interesting him in her affairs, Tony cleared a pretty spot on the grove for the burying-ground, and made ready some small bits of slate on which to write the names of those who died. He did not have it ready an hour too soon, for at sunset two little graves were needed, and Nurse Nelly shed tender tears for her first losses as she laid the motherless mice in one smooth hollow, and the gray-coated rebel in the other. She had learned to care for him already, and when she found him dead, was very glad she had been kind to him, hoping that he knew it, and died happier in her hospital than all alone in the shadowy wood.

The rest of Nelly's patients prospered, and of the many added afterward few died, because of Tony's skillful treatment and her own faithful care. Every morning when the day proved fair the little ambulance went out upon its charitable errand; every afternoon Nelly worked for the human sufferers whom she loved; and every evening brother Will read aloud to her from useful books, showed her wonders with his microscope, or prescribed remedies for the patients, whom he soon knew by name and took much interest in. It was Nelly's holiday; but, though she studied no lessons, she learned much, and unconsciously made her pretty play both an example and a rebuke for others.

At first it seemed a childish pastime, and people laughed. But there was something in the familiar words "Sanitary," "hospital," and "ambulance" that made them pleasant sounds to many ears. As reports of Nelly's work went through the neighborhood, other children came to see and copy her design. Rough lads looked ashamed when in her wards they found harmless creatures hurt by them, and going out they said among themselves, "We won't stone birds, chase butterflies, and drown the girls' little cats any more, though we won't tell them so." And most of the lads kept their word so well that people said there never had been so many birds before as all that summer haunted wood and field. Tender-hearted playmates brought their pets to be cured; even busy fathers had a friendly word for the small charity, which reminded them so sweetly of the great one which should never be forgotten; lonely mothers sometimes looked out with wet eyes as the little ambulance went by, recalling thoughts of absent sons who might be journeying painfully to some far-off hospital, where brave women waited to tend them with hands as willing, hearts as tender, as those the gentle child gave to her self-appointed task.

At home the charm worked also. No more idle days for Nelly, or fretful ones for Will, because the little sister would not neglect the helpless creatures so dependent upon her, and the big brother was ashamed to complain after watching the patience of these lesser sufferers, and merrily said he would try to bear his own wound as quietly and bravely as the "Commodore" bore his. Nelly never knew how much good she had done Captain Will till he went away again in the early autumn. Then he thanked her for it, and though she cried for joy and sorrow she never forgot it, because he left something behind him which always pleasantly reminded her of the double success her little hospital had won.

When Will was gone and she had prayed softly in her heart that God would keep him safe and bring him home again, she dried her tears and went away to find comfort in the place where he had spent so many happy hours with her. She had not been there before that day, and when she reached the door she stood quite still and wanted very much to cry again, for something beautiful had happened. She had often asked Will for a motto for her hospital, and he had promised to find her one. She thought he had forgotten it; but even in the hurry of that busy day he had found time to do more than keep his word, while Nelly sat indoors, lovingly brightening the tarnished buttons on the blue coat that had seen so many battles.

Above the roof, where the doves cooed in the sun, now rustled a white flag with the golden "San. Com." shining on it as the west wind tossed it to and fro. Below, on the smooth panel of the door, a skilful pencil had drawn two arching ferns, in whose soft shadow, poised upon a mushroom, stood a little figure of Nurse Nelly, and underneath it another of Dr. Tony bottling medicine, with spectacles upon his nose. Both hands of the miniature Nelly were outstretched, as if beckoning to a train of insects, birds, and beasts, which was so long that it not only circled round the lower rim of this fine sketch, but dwindled in the distance to mere dots and lines. Such merry conceits as one found there! A mouse bringing the tail it had lost in some cruel trap, a dor-bug with a shade over its eyes, an invalid butterfly carried in a tiny litter by long-legged spiders, a fat frog with gouty feet hopping upon crutches, Jenny Wren sobbing in a nice handkerchief, as she brought dear dead Cock Robin to be restored to life. Rabbits, lambs, cats, calves, and turtles, all came trooping up to be healed by the benevolent little maid who welcomed them so heartily.

Nelly laughed at these comical mites till the tears ran down her cheeks, and thought she never could be tired of looking at them. But presently she saw four lines clearly printed underneath her picture, and her childish face grew sweetly serious as she read the words of a great poet, which Will had made both compliment and motto:

"He prayeth best who loveth best
All things, both great and small;
For the dear God who loveth us,
He made and loveth all."

COLORED SOLDIERS' LETTERS

 D E A R Commonwealth:—As every one is, or ought to be, interested in the efforts now being made for the education of colored persons, old and young, I venture to think that the accompanying letters from several members of one of the colored regiments lately in camp at Readville, will prove interesting to some of your readers as proofs of what a few months of faithful teaching can do for the men, who, with Testament and Primer in their knapsacks, cheerfully shoulder their muskets and march away to fight for a country that disowns them and grudgingly pays for the lives they give in the defence of our liberties as well as their own.

The young lady to whom the letters were written by grateful ex-pupils, tells me that none of them could read, write or spell, when the class was formed; when it was broken up by orders to march, all could read more or less fluently, many could spell as correctly as half our so-called educated boys and girls, and I can testify that the handwriting of the half dozen letters in my possession is in some cases excellent, in no case as unreadable as certain specimens of illustrious illegibility with which most of us are familiar. All errors of spelling, punctuation and grammar have been preserved for the truth's sake, because a few months of care, however heartily bestowed, cannot repair the neglect of years, while the inaccuracies and inelegancies contrasting with the honest and manly sentiments of a great need, but prove how deep a wrong is committed in denying the black man an equal education with the white.

The first letter is dated

> "in Camp Near Citty Point.

"Dear Lady:—I have just Come off pickit duty in the woods and altho very tired and sleepy I feel so happy at receiving your kind letter that I can take no rest untill I have written you a few lines to inform you that we are mostly well. we have only one man that is very sick and he is S. P. one of

From the *Commonwealth* 3, no. 44 (July 1, 1864).

your scholars. he has bin made sick by lying on the ground. We had a small fight on Sunday the 29th of may. it was not very much but anough to let the Rebs or any one Else know that the —— Man is not to be fooled with. no indeed we came from the old Bay state & we are not going to do any thing that will make the blush of shame come upon the face of dear Good Governor Andrews or any of our Good friends at home sweet home the name never had such a sweet sound before as it has now but enough of sentement. now is the time for action. we are as buzzy as bees through-ing up Earth works as the Rebs are very near. the firing this morning was very heavy we could see the flush of Guns and the Bomb shells flying through the air like lighted candles. I am sorry to say that Company ——has lost one of their corporals. he was on pickit duty and got outside the lines by some means or other & was mistaken for a Reb by the sentinell on that post who fired on him and shot him through the thigh of which wound he died this morning. I rejoice with Miss C for the safe return of her brother home from the wars will my poor sister ever have the same cause to rejoice that she has—God knows best—I hope you and yours are all injoying the greatest of all Earthly blessings good health. that you are is the cincear wish of your very humble servant.   H. C.

"Excuse this poor appology for a letter but the fact is there is so much firing bugles sounding men running to and from that a person cannot compose his mind to write. T. M. sends his respects to you and all his teachers."

The next letter is a most imposing document in the original, well writ-ten on a sheet of fools'-cap, expressed with some elegance, and scaled with a thick splash of red wax evidently stamped with a thumb. Not a bad device for a man whose first and perhaps only chance of winning a name lies in the speed and accuracy with which that stout thumb can pull a trigger.

"Dear Madam:—Through the politeness of my first sergeant, I sit down to fulfill a promise made you on the eve of my departure from Readville.

"The evening of the day we left found us embarked on board of a boat at New London, Conn. The next morning we were in New York where we re-embarked for Amboy, N.J. Arrived there about three P.M. we proceeded by rail to Washington, Via Philadelphia and Baltimore. We were sent to Camp Stoneman, six miles from Washington, where we remained for a few days. We were soon dismounted and sent to Camp Casey, located on old General Lee's farm. One night there and we were ordered to report to

Gen. Butler, City Point. We started at once by water and were two days and three nights on the journey.

"We found ourselves in the vicinity of rebeldom on the 14th inst., and had not been there two hours before we were drawn up in line of battle. It appeared that our pickets had been driven in by the rebels inconsiderable force, and it was presumed that they might be in sufficient numbers to make an attack upon us with a promise of success. No demonstration was made, however, and although the troops have been chafing for battle their desire has not yet been gratified.

"We are within hearing of Gen. Butler's guns against Fort Darling and can frequently see the shells burst. We were aroused from our slumbers on the night of the 21st by heavy cannonading up the river and were drawn up in line of battle and remained there till morning. I found that rebels were attempting to send a flat down the river for the purpose of attacking us, but were caught by some of Gen. Butler's gunboats and re-pulsed with a loss of fifteen hundred killed and wounded. Our loss was two killed and three wounded.

"We are drawn up every morning in line of battle and remain so from three A.M. till seven P.M. Our position is well defended by both nature and art. We are protected on two sides by the James River, and on the greater part of the remaining sides by a deep marshy ravine, filled with fallen trees and other obstructions, and exposed to the fire of the Union gunboat fleet, would make our position almost inaccessible from that direction.

"But I have not the time to give you a description of all I see that interests me, but you may expect to hear from the pen of Sergeant P. some correspondence in some of the popular journals that will post you upon the more minute details.

"I have been in good health and fine spirits ever since I left Readville; but even during our most exciting moments I frequently think of those whom I left behind me, whose images, as my imagination pictures them, always recall pleasant moments. I shall be highly gratified to hear from you as often as convenient, and shall write as often as opportunity will allow.

"I have grown heavier and larger since I left Mars, and am impressed with the belief that this climate will do much toward my physical development. Give my love to Miss N. and reserve a share for yourself.

Yours, truly,   S. J."

If space permitted I should be strongly tempted to add, as a pendant to this letter, one lately received from a white soldier, now a student in one of our Western colleges, which has refused to grant a colored student the honors he had won. In which case the white man would be worsted, for "S. J." with his "troops chafing for battle," his positions "well defended by both nature and art," and his impressions regarding his "physical development" entirely outdoes his more fortunate countryman.

The last letter begins in a somewhat novel manner.

"Miss, Permit me through the columns of this letter to write you a few lines to inform you that I am well and hopping this may find you in the same. This present finds me on the sackred soil of Virginia. We are only twenty-six miles from Richmond on the James River. The first day we arrived we thought we would have a battle but we did not; but they are fighting about fifteen miles from here, and we can hear heavy firing almost every minute.

"I am almost through my primer. I say my lesson in my Testament when I have time. We have to sleep on our muskets with our equipments on, and have to git up at three o'clock. If I send you a hundred dollars will you take care of it for me? C. A. sends his respects and said he has not done much toward his book, but has done all he could. Miss W., I hope I may have a chance to come back and have you to teach me some more. I will send you this gold dollar for a present, perhaps when I come home I will be able to give you something worth while speaking of. No more at present, but I have the honor to subscribe your most obedient servant.

T. M."

No, good and grateful "T. M." I think you will find nothing more precious to offer your teacher than the little gold dollar, because the gratitude, affection and respect of which it is the symbol, make it one of those treasures which do not take to themselves wings and fly away. Nor is the ill-spelt but hearty letter valueless, for though sleeping on the "sackred soil of Virginia" with his musket for a pillow, this book-loving "T. M." finds time to get almost through his primer, to read his Testament when he can, and say a friendly word for poor C. A., who has not been able "to do much toward the book" which has been so long in doing anything "toward" him. Let us hope that both may prosper in the double battle they must fight against treason and ignorance, and "have a chance to come back" to the same gentle teaching which has already done so much for them.

Many touching incidents might be related of these men; the hunger for learning which kept some of them poring over books by fire light when the day's duties were done; the eagerness with which an especial gift for mathematics was pursued till its possessor outstripped his accomplished teacher; the pathetic patience with which the dullest plodded on till kindly sympathy and perseverance warmed the benumbed intellect into life and made the soldier twice a man; and more than all, the beautiful respect, the native courtesy, the unspeakable gratitude which found expression in acts that both surprised and touched the receiver. To any who find time hangs heavy on their hands, who have a prejudice to conquer, or who long to help on the great transition, we would say, become a teacher in the Readville barracks and earn a lasting satisfaction through the duties and the pleasures of a just work generously performed.

L.M.A.

AN HOUR

*T*HE clock struck eleven.

"Look again, Gabriel; is there no light coming?"

"Not a ray, mother, and the night seems to darken every instant."

"Surely, half an hour is time enough to reach the main land and find Dr. Firth."

"Ample time; but Alec probably found the doctor absent, and is waiting for him."

"But I bade the boy leave my message, and return at once. Every moment is precious; what can we do?"

"Nothing but wait."

An impatient sigh was the only answer vouchsafed to the unpalatable advice, and silence fell again upon the anxious watchers in the room. Still leaning in the deep recess of the window, the young man looked out into the murky night, listened to the flow of the great river rolling to the sea, and let the unquiet current of his thoughts drift him whithersoever it would. His imaginative temperament found a sad similitude between the night and his own mood, for neither his physical nor mental eye could see what lay before him, and in his life there seemed to have come an hour as full of suspense, as prophetic of storm, as that which now oppressed the earth and lowered in the sky.

Every instant that brought the peace of death nearer to the father, also brought the cares of life nearer to the son, and their grim aspect daunted him. The child of a Northern mother, bred at the North by her dying desire, he had been summoned home to take the old man's place, and receive a slave-cursed inheritance into his keeping. Had he stood alone, his task would have been an easy one; for an upright nature, an enthusiastic spirit, would have found more sweetness than bitterness in a sacrifice made for conscience sake, more pride than pain in a just deed generously performed. But a step-mother and her daughters were dependent on him

Originally published in the *Commonwealth* 3, nos. 13 and 14 (November and December 1864). Reprinted in *Hospital Sketches and Camp and Fireside Stories,* 1869.

now, for the old man's sudden seizure left him no time to make provision for them; and the son found a double burden laid upon his shoulders when he returned to what for years had been a loveless home to him. To reduce three delicately nurtured women to indigence seemed a cruel and Quixotic act to others, a very hard, though righteous one to him; for poverty looked less terrible than affluence founded upon human blood and tears. He had resolved to set aside all private ambitions and aspirations that he might dedicate his life to his kindred; had manfully withstood their ridicule and reproaches, and only faltered when, in their hour of bereavement, they appealed to him with tears and prayers. Then pity threatened to conquer principle, for Gabriel's heart was as gentle as it was generous. Three days of sorrowful suspense and inward strife had passed; now death seemed about to set its seal upon one life, and irresolution to mar another, for Gabriel still wavered between duty and desire, crying within himself, "Lord, help me! I see the right, but I am not strong enough to do it; let it be decided for me."

It was—suddenly, entirely, and forever!

The tinkle of a bell roused him from his moody reverie, and, without quitting the shadow of the half-drawn curtain, he watched the scene before him with the interest of one in whom both soul and sense were alert to interpret and accept the divine decree which he had asked, in whatever guise it came.

The bell summoned a person whose entrance seemed to bring warmth, vitality and light into that gloomy room, although she was only a servant, with the blood of a despised race in her veins. More beautiful than either of her young mistresses, she looked like some brilliant flower of the tropics beside two pale exotics, and the unavoidable consciousness of this showed itself in the skill with which she made her simple dress a foil to her beauty, in the carriage of her graceful head and the sad pride of her eyes, as if, being denied all the other rights of womanhood, the slave clung to and cherished the one possession which those happier women lacked. As she entered, noiselessly, she gave one keen, comprehensive glance about the room,—a glance that took in the gray head and pallid face upon the pillow, the languid lady sitting at the bedside, the young sisters spent with weeping and watching, half asleep in either corner of a couch, and the man's glove that lay beside a brace of pistols on a distant table. Then her eyes fell, all expression faded from her face, and she stood before her mistress with a meek air, curiously at variance with the animated aspect she had worn on entering.

"Milly, are you sure you gave Alec my message correctly?" asked Mrs. Butler, imperiously, with a look of unconcealed dislike.

"Yes, missis, I gave it word for word."

The voice that answered would have gone straight to a stranger's heart and made it ache, for a world of hopeless patience rendered its music pathetic, and dignified the little speech, as if the woman's spirit uttered a protest in every word that passed her lips.

"He has been gone nearly an hour. I can wait no longer. Tell Andy to go at once and see what keeps him."

"Andy's down at the landing, seeing to the boats before the storm, missis."

"Let Tony do that, and send Andy off at once."

"Tony's too cut up with his last whipping to stir."

"How very tiresome! Where is overseer Neal?"

"Sick, missis."

"Sick! I saw him two hours ago, and he was perfectly well then."

"He was taken very suddenly, but he'll be out of pain by morning."

As Milly spoke, with a slight motion of the lips that would have been a scornful smile had she not checked it, a faint, far-off cry came on the wind; a cry of mortal fear or pain it seemed, and so full of ominous suggestion that, though inured to sounds of suffering, Mrs. Butler involuntarily exclaimed,—

"What is that?"

"It's only Rachel screaming for her baby; the last thing old master did was to sell it, and she's been crazy ever since," answered Milly, with a peculiar quickening of the breath and a sidelong glance.

"Foolish creature! but never mind her now: tell me who is about that I can send for Dr. Firth."

"There's no one in the house but blind Sandra and me."

"What do you mean? Who gave the people leave to go?"

"I did."

Hitherto the girl had spoken in the subdued tone of a well-trained servant, though there was no trace of her race in her speech but a word or two here and there; for Milly's beauty had secured for her all the advantages which would increase her value as a chattel. But in the utterance of the last two words her voice rose with a sudden ring that arrested Mrs. Butler's attention, and caused her to glance sharply at the girl. Milly stood before her meek and motionless, and not an eyelash stirred during that brief scrutiny. Her mistress could not see the mingled triumph and abhorrence burning in those averted eyes, did not observe the close clenching of the hand that hung at her side, nor guess what a sea of black and bitter memories was surging in her comely hand-maid's heart.

"How dared you send the servants away without my orders?" demanded Mrs. Butler, in an irritated and irritating voice.

"Master Gabriel said the house must be kept very quiet on old master's account; I couldn't make the boys mind, so I sent them to the quarters."

"This is not the first time you have presumed upon my son's favor, and exceeded my orders. You have been spoiled by indulgence, but that shall be altered soon."

"Yes, missis,—it shall;" and as the girl added the latter words below her breath, there was a glitter as of white teeth firmly set lest some impetuous speech should break loose in spite of her. Her mistress did not mark that little demonstration, for her mind was occupied with its one care, as she said, half aloud, half to herself,—

"What shall I do? The night is passing, your master needs help, and Alec has evidently forgotten, or never received, my message."

For the first time an expression of anxiety was visible on Milly's face, and there was more eagerness than deference in her suggestion:

"Master Gabriel might go; it would save time and make the matter sure, as missis doubts my word."

"It is impossible; his father might rouse and ask for him, and I will not be left alone. It is not his place to carry messages, nor yours to propose it. Quick! lift your master's head, and chafe his hands. God help us all!"

A low sigh from the bed caused the sudden change from displeasure to distress, as Mrs. Butler bent over her husband, forgetful of all else. What a strange smile flashed across Milly's face, and kindled the dark fire of her eyes, as she looked down upon the master and mistress, whose helplessness and grief touched no chord of pity or sympathy in her heart! Only an instant did she stand so, but in that instant the expression of her face was fully revealed, not to the drowsy sisters, but to Gabriel in his covert. He saw it, but before he could fathom its significance it was hidden from him; and when his mother looked up there was nothing to be seen but the handsome head bending over the pale hand that Milly was assiduously chafing. Something in the touch of those warm palms seemed to rouse in the old man a momentary flicker of memory and strength, for the last thought that had disturbed his failing consciousness found utterance in broken words:

"I promised her her liberty,—she shall have it; wait a little, Milly,—wait till I am better."

"Yes, master, I can wait now;" and the girl's eye turned toward the clock with an impatient glance.

The old man did not hear her, for, with an incoherent murmur, he seemed to sink into a deeper lethargy than before. His wife believed him dying; and cried, as she wrung her hands in a paroxysm of despairing helplessness,—

"Look out, Milly, look out! and if no one is coming, run to the quarters and send off the first boy you meet."

Milly moved deliberately toward the window, but paused half-way to ask, with the same shade of anxiety flitting over her face,—

"Where is Master Gabriel? shouldn't he be called?"

"He was here a moment ago, and has gone to the landing, doubtless; you can call him as you go."

With sudden eagerness the girl glided to the window, now too intent upon some purpose of her own to see the dark outline of a figure half concealed in the deep folds of the curtain; and, leaning far out, she peered into the gloom with an intentness that sharpened every feature.

"There is no one coming, missis," she said, raising her voice unnecessarily, as one listener thought, unless the momentary stillness made any sound seem unusually loud. As the words left her lips, from below there came a soft chirp as of some restless bird; it was twice repeated, then came a pause, and in it, with a rapid, noiseless gesture, Milly drew a handkerchief from her pocket and dropped it from the window. It fluttered whitely for a moment, and as it disappeared an acute ear might have caught the sound of footsteps stealing stealthily away. Milly evidently heard them, for an expression of relief began to dawn upon her face. Suddenly it changed to one of terror, as, in the act of withdrawing her arm, a strong hand grasped it, and Gabriel's voice demanded,—

"What does this mean, Milly?"

For a moment she struggled like some wild creature caught in a net, then steadied herself by a desperate effort, exclaiming, breathlessly,—

"Oh, Master Gabriel, how you frightened me!"

"I meant to. Now tell what all this means, at once and truly," he said, in a tone intended to be stern, but which was only serious and troubled.

"All what means, sir?" she answered, feigning innocent surprise, though her eye never met his, and she still trembled in his hold.

"You know; the signals, the dropping of the handkerchief, the steps below there, and the figure creeping through the grass."

"Master must have quick eyes and ears to see and hear all that in such a minute. I only saw my handkerchief drop by accident; I only heard a bird chirp, and one of the dogs creep round the house;" but as she spoke she cast an uneasy glance over her shoulder into the night without.

"Why lie to me, Milly? I have watched you ever since you came in, and you are not yourself to-night. Something is wrong; I've felt it all day, but thought it was anxiety for my poor father. Why are all the people sent off to the quarters? Why is Andy meddling with the boats without my orders? and why do you look, speak, and act in this inexplicable manner?"

"If master gets worried and imagines mischief when there is none, I can't help it," she said, doggedly.

Both while speaking and listening Gabriel had scrutinized her closely, and all he saw confirmed his suspicion that something serious was amiss. In the slender wrist he held the pulse thrilled quick and strong; he heard the rapid beating of her heart, the flutter of the breath upon her lips; saw that her face was colorless, her eyes both restless and elusive. He was sure that no transient fear agitated her, but felt that some unwonted excitement possessed her, threatening to break out in spite of the self-control which years of servitude had taught her. What he had just seen and heard alarmed him; for his father had been a hard master, the island was governed by fear alone, and he never trod the dykes that bounded the long, low rice-fields without feeling as if he walked upon a crater-crust, which might crack and spew fire any day. Many small omens of evil had occurred of late, which now returned to his recollection with sinister significance; and the vague disquiet that had haunted him all day now seemed an instinctive premonition of impending danger. Many fears flashed through his mind, and one resolution was firmly fixed. His face grew stern, his voice commanding, and his hand tightened its hold as he said,—

"Speak, Milly, or I shall be tempted to use my authority as a master, and that I never wish to do. If there is any deviltry afloat I must know it; and if you will not tell it me I shall search the island till I find it for myself."

She looked at him for the first time, as he spoke, with a curious blending of defiance for the master and admiration for the man. His last words changed it to one of fear; and her free hand was extended as if to bar his way, while she said, below her breath, and with another glance into the outer gloom,—

"You are safe here, but if you leave the house it will cost you your life."

"Then it must; for if you will not show me the peril, I swear I'll go to meet it blindly."

"No, no, wait a little; I dare not tell!"

"You shall tell. I am the mistress here, and have borne enough. Speak, girl, at once, or this proud spirit of yours shall be broken till you do."

Mrs. Butler had heard all that passed, had approached them, and being a woman who was by turns imperious, peevish, and passionate, she yielded to the latter impulse as she spoke, and gave the girl's shoulder an impatient shake, as if to force the truth out of her. The touch, the tone, were like sparks to powder; for the smouldering fire blazed up as Milly flung her off, wrenched herself free from Gabriel, and turned on his mother with a look that sent her back to her husband trembling and dismayed.

"Yes, I will speak, though it is too soon!" cried Milly, with a short, sharp laugh. "They may kill me for telling before the time; I can't help it; I must have one hour of freedom, if I die the next. There *is* deviltry afloat tonight, and it is yourselves you may blame for it. We can't bear any more, and before a new master comes to torment us like the old one, we've determined to try for liberty, though there'll be bloody work before we get it. The boys are not at the quarters, but fifty are waiting at the rice-mill till midnight, and then they'll come up here to do as they've been done by. While they wait they're beginning with overseer Neal; whipping, burning, torturing him, for all I know, as other men, and women too, have been whipped, burnt and tortured there. That was his scream you heard. Alec never went for the doctor; Andy's guarding the boats till we want them; big Mose is watching round the house; the alarm bell's down; I've cleared the house of arms, and spoilt the pistols that I dared not take; Master Gabriel's the only white man on the island, and there's no help for you unless the Lord turns against us. Who is the mistress now?"

The girl paused there, breathless but exultant, for the words had poured from her lips as if the pent-up degradation, wrath and wrong of nineteen years had broken bounds at last and must overflow, even though they wrecked her by their vehemence. Some spirit stronger than herself seemed to possess and speak out of her, making her look like an embodied passion, beautiful, yet terrible, as she glanced from face to face, seeing how pale and panic-stricken each became, as her rapid words made visible the retribution that hung over them. Gabriel stood aghast at the swift and awful answer given to his prayer; the daughters fled to their mother's arms for shelter; the wife clung to her husband for the protection which he could no longer give, and, as if dragged back to life by the weight of a woe, such as he had himself inflicted upon others, the old man rose up in his bed, speechless, helpless, yet conscious of the dangers of the hour, and doubly daunted by death's terrors, because so powerless to succor those for whom he had periled his own soul. A bitter cry broke from him as his last look showed him the impending doom which all his impotent remorse could not avert, and in that cry the old man's spirit passed, to find that, even for such as he, Infinite justice was tempered by Infinite mercy.

During the few moments in which the wife and daughters forgot fear in sorrow, and the son took hurried counsel with himself how best to meet the coming danger, Milly was learning that the bitter far exceeds the sweet in human vengeance. The slave exulted in the freedom so dearly purchased, but the woman felt that in avenging them her wrongs had lost their dignity, and though she had changed places with her mistress, she found that power did not bring her peace. She had no skill to analyze the feeling, no words in which to express it, even to herself, but she was so strongly conscious of it, that its mysterious power marred the joy she thought to feel, and forced her to confess that in the hour of expected triumph she was baffled and defeated by her own conscience. With women doomed to a fate like hers, the higher the order of intelligence the deeper the sense of degradation, the more intense the yearning for liberty at any price. Milly had always rebelled against her lot, although, compared with that of her class, it had not been a hard one till the elder Butler bought her, that his son, seeing slavery in such a lovely form, might learn to love it. But Gabriel, in his brief visits, soon convinced his father that no temptation could undermine his sturdy Northern sense of right and justice, and though he might easily learn to love the beautiful woman, he could not learn to oppress the slave whose utter helplessness appealed to all that was manliest in him.

Milly felt this deeply, and knew that the few black drops in her veins parted herself and Gabriel more hopelessly than the widest seas that ever rolled between two lovers. This inexorable fact made all the world look dark to her; life became a burden, and one purpose alone sustained her,— the resolution to achieve her own liberty, to enjoy a brief triumph over those who had wronged her, then to die, and find compensation for a hapless human love in the fatherly tenderness of a Divine one. She had prayed, worked and waited for this hour, with all the ardor, energy and patience of her nature. Yet when it came she was not satisfied; a sense of guilt oppressed her, and the loss seemed greater than the gain. Gabriel had given her a look which wounded more deeply than the sharpest reproach; and the knowledge that she had forfeited the confidence he had always shown her, now made her gloomy when she would have been glad, humble when she thought to have been proudest. Gabriel saw and understood her mood, felt that their only hope of deliverance lay in her, and while his mother and sisters lamented for the dead, he bestirred himself to save the living.

"Milly," he began, with sad seriousness, "we deserve no mercy, and I ask none for myself; I only implore you to spare the women and give me time to atone for the weak, the wicked hesitation which has brought us to this pass. I meant to free you all as soon as you were legally mine, as it was too late for my father to endear his memory by one just act. But it was hard to make my mother and my sisters poor, and so I waited, hoping to be shown some way by which I could be just and generous both to you and them."

"Three women were more precious than two hundred helpless creatures in the eyes of a Christian gentleman from the free North! I'm glad you told me this;" and there was something like contempt in the look she gave her master.

There was no answer to that, for it was true; and in the remorseful shame that sent the blood to Gabriel's forehead, he confessed the fact which he was too honest to deny. Still looking at her, with eyes that pleaded for him better than his words, he said, with a humility that conquered her disdain,—

"I shall expiate that sin if I die to-night; and I will give myself up to be dealt with as you please, if you will save my mother and my sisters, and let them free you in my name. Before God and my dead father I promise this, upon my honor!"

"There are no witnesses to that but those whom I'll not trust; honor means nothing to us who are not allowed to keep our own," said Milly, looking moodily upon the ground, as if she feared to look up lest she should relent, for excitement was ebbing fast, and a flood of regretful recollections rising in her heart.

"I did not expect that reproach from you," Gabriel answered, taking courage from the signs he saw. "Do you remember, when my father gave you to me, how indignantly I rejected the gift, and promised that in my eyes you should be as sacred as either of those poor girls? Have I not kept my word, Milly?"

"Yes! O yes!" she said, with trembling lips, and eyes she dared not lift, they were so full of grateful tears. Carefully steadying her traitorous voice, she added, earnestly, "Master Gabriel! I *do* remember, and I've tried all day to save you, but you wouldn't go. I will trust your word, and do my best to help the ladies, if they'll promise to free us all to-morrow, and you will leave the island at once. Mose will let you pass; for that handkerchief was dropped to tell him that you were abroad, and were to be got off against your will, if you wouldn't go quietly. Both he and Andy will save you for my sake; the others won't, because they don't know you as we do. Please go, Master Gabriel, before it is too late."

"No, I shall stay. What would you think of me, if I deserted these helpless women in such danger, to save myself at their expense? I cannot quite trust you, Milly, after treachery like this."

"Who taught us to be treacherous, and left us nothing but our own cunning to help ourselves with?"

The first part of Gabriel's speech made the last less hard to bear; and Milly's question was put in a tone that was more apologetic than accusatory, for Gabriel cared what she thought of him, and that speech comforted her.

"Not I, Milly; but let the sins of the dead rest, and tell me if you will not help my mother and Grace and Clara off, instead of me? The promise will be all the sooner and the better kept, or, if it comes too late, I shall be the only and the fittest person to pay the penalty."

Milly's face darkened, and she turned away with an expression of keen disappointment. Mrs. Butler and her daughters had restrained their lamentations to listen; but at the sound of Gabriel's proposal, the sisters ran to Milly, and, clinging about her knees, implored her to pity, forgive, and save them. Well for them that they did so; for Milly felt as if many degradations were cancelled by that act, and, as she saw her young mistresses at her feet, the sense of power soothed her sore heart, and added the grace of generosity to the duty of forgiveness. She did not speak, yet she did not deny their prayer, and stood wavering between doubt and desire as the fateful moments rapidly flew by; Gabriel remembered that, and, taking her hand, said, in a voice whose earnestness was perilously persuasive to the poor girl's ear,—

"Milly, you said there was no hope for us unless God turned against you. I think He has, and, speaking through that generous heart of yours, pleads for us better than we can plead for ourselves. It is so beautiful to pity, so magnanimous to forgive; and the greater the wrong, the more pardon humbles the transgressor and ennobles the bestower. Dear Milly, spare these poor girls as you have been spared; prove yourself the truer woman, the nobler mistress; teach them a lesson which they never can forget, and sweeten your liberty with the memory of this act."

Milly listened still with downcast eyes and averted face, but every word went straight to her heart, soothing, strengthening, inspiring all that was best and bravest in that poor heart, so passionate, and yet so warm and womanly withal. No man had ever spoken to her before of magnanimity, of proving herself superior to those who had shown no mercy to her faults, accorded no praise to her virtues, nor lightened a hard servitude with any touch of friendliness. No man had ever looked into her face before with eyes in which admiration for her beauty was mingled with pity for her helpless womanhood; and, better than all, no man, old or young, had ever until now recognized in her a fellow-creature, born to the same rights, gifted with the same powers, and capable of the same sufferings and sacrifices as himself. That touched and won her; that appealed to the spirit which lives through all oppression in the lowest of God's children; and through all her frame there went a glow of warmth and joy, as if some strong, kind hand had lifted her from the gloom of a desolate despair into the sunshine of a happier world. Her eye wandered toward the faces of dead master, conquered mistress, and darkened as it looked; passed to the pale girls still clinging to her skirts, and softened visibly; was lifted to Gabriel, and kindled with the new-born desire to prove herself worthy of the confidence which would be her best reward. A smile broke beautifully across her face, and her lips were parted to reply, when Mrs. Butler, who sat trembling behind her, cried, in a shrill, imploring whisper,—

"Remember all I've done for you, Milly, all I still have it in my power to do. I promise to free you, if you will only save us now. Be merciful, for your old master's sake, if not for mine."

The sound of that querulous voice seemed to sting Milly like a lash, threatening to undo all Gabriel's work. Her eye grew fiery again, her mouth hard, her face bitterly scornful, as she said, with a glance which her mistress never forgot,—

"I'm not likely to forget all you've done for me; I would not accept my liberty from you if you could give it; and if a word of mine could save you, I'd not say it for old master's sake, much less for yours."

With a warning gesture to his mother, Gabriel turned that defiant face toward himself, and holding it firmly yet gently between his hands, bent on it a look that allayed the rising storm by the magic of a power which the young man had never used till now, though conscious of possessing it,—for Milly's tell-tale countenance had betrayed her secret long ago. As he looked deep into her eyes, with a glance which was both commanding and compassionate, they first fell with sudden shame, then, as if controlled by the power of those other eyes, they rose again and met them with a sad sincerity that made their beauty tragical, as they filled slowly till two great tears rolled down her cheeks, wetting the hands that touched them; and when Gabriel said, softly, "For my sake you will save us?" she straightway answered, "Yes."

"God bless you, Milly! Now tell me how I am to help you, for time is going, and lives hang on the minutes."

He released her as he spoke; and, though she still looked at him as if he were the one saving power of her thwarted life, she answered, pleadingly,—

"Hush, Master Gabriel! please don't speak to me, for then I only feel,—now I must think."

How still the room grew as they waited ! The presence of death was less solemn than that of fear, for the dead seemed forgotten, and the living all unconscious of the awesome contrast between the pale expectancy of their panic-stricken faces and the repose of that one untroubled countenance. How suddenly the night grew full of ominous sounds! How intently all eyes were fixed upon the beautiful woman who stood among them holding their lives in her hands, and how they started, when, through the hush, came a soft chime as the half-hour struck! Milly heard and answered that silvery sound as the anxious watchers would have had her:

"It can be done," she said, in a tone which carried hope to every heart. "It can be done, but I must do it alone, for I can pass Mose and get Andy across the river without their suspecting that I'm going for help. You must stay here and do your best to guard the ladies, Master Gabriel; it won't be safe for any of you to go now."

"But, Milly, the boys may not wait till twelve, or you may be delayed, and then we are lost."

"I have thought of that; and as I go out I'll take old Sandra with me; she'll understand in a minute. She'll go down to the mill and talk to them and keep them, if anything can do it, for they love and fear her more than any one on the island. Be quiet, trust to me, and I'll save you, Master Gabriel."

He silently held out his hand, as if pledging his word to obey and trust. With the warmth and grace of her impulsive temperament, Milly bent her head, laid her cheek against that friendly hand, wet it with grateful tears, kissed it with loving lips, and went her way, feeling as if all things were possible to her for Gabriel's sake.

Listening breathlessly, they heard her foot-falls die away, heard Sandra's voice below, a short parley with Mose, then watched the old woman and the young depart in opposite directions, leaving them to feel the bitterness of dependence in a strange, stern fashion, which they had never thought to know. Man-like, Gabriel could not long stand idle while danger menaced and women faced it for him. Anxious to take such precautions as might hold the expected assailants at bay, even for a moment, he bade his mother and sisters remain quiet, that no suspicion might be excited, and crept down to test the capabilities of the house to withstand a short siege, if other hopes failed. The slight, many-doored and windowed mansion, built for a brief occupancy when the winter months rendered the region habitable for whites, was but ill-prepared to repel any attack; and a hasty survey convinced Gabriel that it was both hazardous and vain to attempt a barricade which a few strong arms could instantly destroy. As he stood disheartened, unarmed, and alone in the long hall, dimly lighted by the lamp he carried, a sense of utter desolation came over him, dampening his courage, and oppressing his mind with the dreariest forebodings. Thinking of the many true hearts and stout arms far away there at the North, which would have come to his aid so readily could his need have been known, he yearned for a single friend, a single weapon, that he might conquer or die like a man. And both were given him.

Pausing before a door that opened out upon the rear of the house, his eye caught sight of a heavy whip, whose loaded handle had felled men before now, and might easily do so again, if wielded by a strong arm. He took it down, saying to himself, "It is the first time I ever touched the accursed thing; God grant that it may be the last." A low sound behind him caused the blood to chill an instant in his veins, then to rush on with a quicker flow, as, poising the weapon in one hand, he lifted the lamp upon his head, and searched the gloom. Far at the other end of the long hall a dark figure crept along, and a pair of glittering eyes were fixed upon his own. "Come on; I'm ready," he said, steadily, and was answered by the patter of rapid steps, the sight of an unexpected ally, as a great black hound came leaping upon him in a rapture of canine delight. Old Mort had been the fiercest, most efficient blood-hound on the island; and still, in spite of age, was a formidable beast, ready to track or assault a negro, and pull him down or throttle him, at word of command. He had been his possessor's favorite till Gabriel came; then he deserted the old master for the young, and was always left at large when he was at home. Mort had been missing all day, and now the rope trailing behind him was sufficient evidence that he had been decoyed away, lest his vigilance should warn his master, and that, having freed himself, he had stolen home, to lie concealed till night and his master's presence reassured him.

As the great creature reared himself before the young man, with a paw on either shoulder, and looked into his face with eyes that seemed almost human in their intelligent affection, Gabriel dropped the whip, put down the lamp, and caressed the hound with an almost boyish gratitude and fondness; for, with the sense of security this powerful ally brought, there came a remorseful memory, that, though the possessor of two hundred human beings, he had no friend but a dog. At this point Mort suddenly pricked up his ears, slipped from his master's hold, and snuffed suspiciously at the closed door. Some one was evidently without, and the creature's keen scent detected the unseen listener. With a noiseless command to the dog to keep quiet, Gabriel caught up his only weapon, and stood waiting for whatever demonstration should follow. None came; and presently Mort returned to him with a sagacious glance and a sleepy yawn, sure evidences that Mose had paused a moment in his round, and had gone on again. Big Mose was, with one exception, the strongest, most rebellious slave on the place; and though Gabriel had longed to rush out and attack him, he had not dared to try it, for his strength was as a child's compared to the stalwart slave's. Now, with Mort to help him, the thing was possible; and as he stood there, with only a door between him and the man who had sworn to take his life, a strange consciousness of power came to him; his muscles seemed to grow firm as iron, his blood flowed calm and cool, and in his mind there rose a purpose, desperately simple, yet wise, despite its seeming rashness. He would master Mose, and, leaving Mort to guard him, would go down to the mill, and, if both Sandra's and his own appeals and promises proved unavailing, would give himself up, hoping that his death or torture would delay the doom of those defenceless women, and give Milly time to bring them better help than any he could give. Some atonement must be made, he thought, and perhaps innocent blood would wash the black stain from his father's memory better than the deed he had hoped to do in that father's name on the morrow. He had held a precious opportunity in his hands, had delayed through a mistaken kindness; now it was lost, perhaps forever, and he must pay the costly price which God exacts of those who palter with their consciences. As the thought came, and the purpose grew, it brought with it that high courage, that entire self-abnegation which we call heroism; and that fateful moment made Gabriel a man.

A word, a gesture, put the dog upon his mettle; then cutting away the long rope, Gabriel threw it over his arm, unbarred the door, set it ajar, and, standing behind it, with the hound under his hand, he waited for Mose to make his round. Soon Mort's restless ears gave token of his approach; and, as the stealthy steps came stealing on, he was with difficulty restrained; for now instinct showed him danger, and he was as eager as his master to be up and doing. The streak of light attracted the man's eye. He paused, drew nearer, listened; then softly pushed the door open, and leaned in to reconnoitre. That instant Mort was on him, a heavy blow half stunned him, and, before his scattered wits could be collected, he was down, his hands fast bound, and both master and dog standing over him panting, but unhurt.

"Now, Mose, if you want to save your life, be still, and answer my questions truly," said Gabriel, with one hand on the man's throat, the other holding back Mort, whose tawny eye was savage now. "I know your plot, and have found means to spoil it. How do you think I'm going to punish you all?"

"Dun'no, massa," muttered Mose, with a grim resignation to any fate.

"I'm going to free every man, woman, and child on the island, and fling that devilish thing into the river," he said, as he spurned the whip with his foot.

An incredulous look and derisive grin was the only thanks and answer he received.

"You don't believe it? Well, who can blame you, poor soul? Not I. Now tell me how many men are on the watch between here and the rice-mill?" Gabriel spoke with a flash of the eye and a sudden deepening of the voice; for both indignation and excitement stirred him. The look, the tone, did more to convince Mose than a flood of words; for he had learned to try men by tests of his own, and had more faith in the promises of their faces than those of their tongues. More respectfully, he said,—

"No one, 'sides me, massa. Andy's at de landin', and de rest at de mill 'ceptin' dem as isn't in de secret."

"Mind, no lies, Mose, or your free papers will be the last I sign to-morrow. Get up, and come quietly with me; for if you try to run, Mort will pin you. I'm going to the mill, and want you safely under lock and key first."

"Is massa gwine alone?" asked Mose, glancing about him, for Gabriel spoke as if he had a score of men at his command.

"Yes, I'm going alone; why not?"

"Massa knows dere's fifty of de boys dar sworn to kill him, if Milly don't git him 'way 'fore dey comes up?"

"I know, and Milly's done her best to get me off, but I'd rather stay; I'm not afraid."

Gabriel's blood was up now: danger had no terrors for him; and, beyond the excitement of the moment, his purpose lent him a calm courage which impressed the slave as something superhuman. Like one in a maze of doubt and fear, he obediently followed his master to an out-house, where, binding feet as well as hands, Gabriel left him with the promise and the warning,—

"Sit here till I come to let you out a free man, if I live to do it. Don't stir nor call, for Mort will be at the door to silence you and howl for me, if you try any tricks. I'll not keep you long, if I can help it."

The slave only stared dumbly at him, incapable of receiving the vast idea of liberty, pardon, and kindness all at once; and bidding Mort guard both prisoner and house, Gabriel stole along the path that wound away through grove and garden to the rice-mill, where so many fates were soon to be decided. As he went he glanced from earth to sky, and found propitious omens everywhere. No flowery thicket concealed a lurking foe to clutch at him in the dark; but the fragrance of trodden grass, the dewy touch of leaves against his cheek, the peaceful night-sounds that surrounded him, gave him strange comfort and encouragement; for when his fellow-creatures had deserted, Nature took him to her motherly heart. From above, fitful glimpses of the moon guided him on his perilous way; for the wind had changed, the black clouds were driving seaward, and the storm was passing without either thunderbolt or hurricane. Coming, at length, within sight of the half-ruined mill, he paused to reconnoitre. Through chinks in the rude walls a dim light shone, and muffled voices rose and fell; and once there was a hoarse sound, as of a half-uttered shout. Creeping warily to a dark nook among the ruins, Gabriel made his way to a crevice in an inner wall, and, looking through it, saw a sight little fitted to reassure him, either as a master or a man.

The long, low-raftered portion of the mill, which once had been the threshing-floor, was now lighted by the red glare of several torches, which filled the place with weird shadows, and sudden glimpses of objects that seemed the more mysterious or terrible for being but half seen. In one corner, under a coarse covering, something lay stark and still; a clenched hand was visible, and several locks of light hair dabbled with blood, but nothing more. Fifty men, old and young, of all shades of color, all types of their unhappy race, stood or sat about three, who evidently were the leaders of the league. One, a young man, so fair that the red lines across his shoulders looked doubly barbarous there, was half-kneeling, and steadily filing at a chain that held his feet together as his hands had been held till some patient friend had freed them, and left him to finish the slow task. He worked so eagerly that the drops stood thick upon his haggard face, and his scarred chest heaved with his painful breath; for this was the Tony who was too much cut up with his last whipping to run on Mrs. Butler's errand, but not too feeble to strike a blow for liberty. The second man was as near an animal as a human creature could become, and yet to be recognized as such. A burly, brutal-looking negro, maimed and distorted by every cruelty that could be invented or inflicted, he was a sight to daunt the stoutest heart, as he sat sharpening the knife which had often threatened him in the overseer's hand, and was still red with the overseer's blood.

Standing erect between the two, and in striking contrast to them, was a gigantic man, with a fine, dark face, a noble head, and the limbs of an ebony Hercules. A native African, from one of those tribes whose wills are never broken,—who can be subdued by kindness, but who often kill themselves rather than suffer the degradation of the lash. No one had dared to subject him to that chastisement, as was proved by the unmarred smoothness of the muscular body, bare to the waist; but round his neck was riveted an iron collar, with four curved spikes. It was a shameful badge of serfdom; it prevented him from lying down, it galled him with its cease-less chafing, yet he wore it with an air which would have made the hid-eous necklace seemed some barbaric ornament, if that had been possible; and faced the excited crowd with a native dignity which nothing could destroy, and which proved him their master in intelligence, as well as strength and courage.

Before them all, yet lifted a little above them by her position on a fallen fragment of the roof, stood old Cassandra. A tall, gaunt woman, with a countenance which age, in making venerable, had not robbed of its vigor; her sightless eyes were wide open with a weird effect of seeing without sight, and her high white turban, her long staff, and the involuntary tremor of her shrivelled hands, gave her the air of some ancient sorceress or priestess, bearing her part in some heathen rite. The majestic-looking slave with the collar had apparently been speaking, for his face was turned toward her, and his dark features were still alive with the emotions which had just found vent in words. As Gabriel looked, old Sandra struck the floor with her staff, as if commanding silence; and, as the stir of some momentary outbreak subsided, she said, in a strong voice, which rose and fell in a sort of solemn chant as her earnestness increased and her listeners grew obedient to its spell,—

"Chil'en, I'se heerd yer plans,—now I wants ter len' a han' and help you in dis hour of tribbleation. You's killed oberseer Neal, and d'rectly you's all gwine up ter de house to kill massa, missis and de young folks. Now what's you gwine to do dat for? and what's dey eber done bad nuf ter make you willin' ter fro 'way yer souls dis night?"

"Kase we can't b'ar no more." "Old massa hunted my boy wid hounds and dey tore him ter def." "He sold my chil'en and drove Rachel crazy wid de partin'." "Old missis had my pore girl whipped kase she was too sick ter stan' and dress her." "Massa Gabriel may be harder dan de ole one, and we's tired ob hell."

These, and many another short, stern answer, came to Sandra's question; she expected them, was ready to meet them, and knew how best to reach the outraged hearts now hungering for vengeance. Her well-known afflictions, her patience, her piety, gave a certain sanctity to her presence, great weight to her words, and an almost marvellous power to her influence over her own people, who believed her to be half saint, half seer. She felt her power, and, guided by an instinct that seldom failed, she used it wisely in this perilous hour, remembering that her listeners, though men in their passions, were children in their feelings.

"You pore boys, I knows de troof ob all dat, and I'se had my trubbles hard and heavy as you has, but I'se learnt to fergib 'em, and dey don't hurt now. Ole massa bought me thirty year' ago 'way from all I keered fer, and I'se slaved for him widout no t'anks, no wages, eber since; but I'se fergived him dat. He sole my chil'en, all ten; my boys up de riber, my perty little girls down to Orleans, and bringed up his chil'en on de money; dat come bery hard, but de Lord helped me, and I fergived him dat. He shot my ole Ben kuse he couldn't whip me hisself, nor stan' by and see it done; dat mos' broke my heart, but in de end I foun' I could fergib him one time more. He made me nuss him when de fever come and every one was 'fraid ob him; de long watchin', de hard work and de cryin' fer my chil'en made me bline at last; but I fergived him dat right hearty, for though dey took my eyes away dey couldn't bline my soul, and in de darkness I hab seen de Lord."

The truth, the pathos, the devout assurance of her words, impressed and controlled the sympathetic creatures to whom she spoke, as no reproach or denunciation would have done. A murmur went through the crowd, and more than one savage face lost something of its brutality, gained something of its former sad patience, as the old woman touched, with wondrous skill, the chords that still made music in these tried and tempted hearts.

"Yes, chil'en, I hab seen de Lord, and He has made de night into day fer me, has held me up in all my trubbles, tole me to hole fas' by Him, and promised He would bring me safe ter glory. I'se faith ter feel He will, and while I wait, I'se savin' up my soul fer Him. Boys, He says de same to you froo me; He says hole fas', b'ar all dat's sent, beleebe in Him, and wait the coming ob de Lord."

"We's done tired a-waitin', de Lord's so bery long a comin', Sandra."

It was a weary, hopeless voice that answered, as an old man shook his white head and lifted up the dim eyes that for eighty years had watched in vain.

"It's you dat's long a-comin' ter Him, Uncle Dave, but He ain't tired ob waitin' for yer. De places dar in heaven is all ready, de shinin' gowns, de harps ob gole, de eberlastin' glory, and de peace. No rice-swamps dar, no sugar-mills, no cotton-fields, no houn's, no oberseer, no massa but de blessed Lord. Dar's yer chil'en, Uncle Dave, growed beautiful white angels, and a-waitin' till yer comes. Dar's yer wife, Pete, wid no lashes on her back, no sobbin' in her heart, a-waiting fer yer, anxious. Dar's yer fader, Jake; he don't need no proppin' now, and he'll run to meet yer when yer comes. Dar's yer pore sister Rachel, Ned; she ain't crying for baby now, de Lord's got her in de holler ob His han', and she's a-waitin' fer de little one and you to come. Dar's my Ben, my chil'en all saved up for me, and when I comes I'll see 'em waitin' fer me at de door. But, best ob all, dar's de dear Lord waitin' fer us; he's holdin' out his arms, He's beckonin' all de while, He's sayin', in dat lovin' voice ob His, 'I sees yer sorrows, my pore chil'en, I hears yer sobbin' and yer prayers, I fergives yer sins, I knows yer won't 'spoint me ob dese yere fifty precious souls, and I'se a-waitin', waitin', waitin' fer yer all.'"

Strange fervor was in the woman's darkened face, strange eloquence in her aged voice, strange power in the persuasive gestures of her withered hands outstretched above them, warning, pleading, beckoning, as if, in truth, the Lord spoke through her, illuminating that poor place with the light of His divine compassion, the promises of His divine salvation. A dead silence followed as the last yearning cadence of the one voice rose, fell, and died away. Sandra let the strong contrast between the here and the hereafter make its due impression, then broke the silence, saying briefly, solemnly,—

"Boys, de Lord has spared yer one great sin dis night; ole massa's dead."

"Glory be to God, amen!" "Halleluyer! dat I'se libed ter see dis happy day!" "De Debble's got him, shore!" "Don't give up de chance, boys; young massa and de missis is lef' for us."

Such exclamations of gratitude, joy, and revenge, were the only demonstration which the news produced, and, mingling with them, a gust of wind came sweeping through the mill, as if nature gave a long sigh of relief that another tyrant had ceased to blight and burden her fair domain. Sandra's quick ear caught the last words, and a deep oath or two, as several men rose with the fierce fire rekindling in their eyes.

"Yes!" she cried, in a tone that held them even against their will,—"yes, young massa's lef'; but not to die, for if yer gives up your chance of damnation dis night, you'll all be free to-morrer. He's promised it; he'll do it, and dere'll be no blood but dat bad man's yonder, to cry from de groun', and b'ar witness 'ginst yer at de Judgment-Day."

"Free! to-morrer! Who's gwine to b'lieve dat, Sandra? We's been tole such stories often; but de morrer's never come, and now we's gwine to bring one for ourselves."

The gigantic man with the spiked collar on his neck said that, with a smile of grim determination, as he took up the iron bar, which in his desperate hands became a terribly formidable weapon.

A low growl, as of muttering thunder, answered him, and Sandra's heart sunk within her. But one hope remained; and, desperately clinging to it, she found that even in these betrayed, benighted creatures there still lived a sense of honor, a loyalty to truth, born of the manhood God had given them, the gratitude which one man had inspired.

"Hear me, jes once more, 'fore yer goes, boys. Tell me, what has young massa done ter make yer want his blood? Has he ever lashed yer, kicked, and cussed yer? Has he sole yer chil'ren, 'bused yer wives, or took yer ole folks from yer? Has he done anything but try to make ole massa kinder, to do his best for us while he's here; and when he can't do nor b'ar no more, don't he go 'way to pray de Lord ter help us fer His sake?"

Not a voice answered; not one complaint, accusation, or reproach was made, and Prince, the fierce leader of the insurrection, paused, with his foot upon the threshold of the door; for a grateful memory confronted and arrested him. One little daughter, the last of many children, had been taken from him to be sold, when Gabriel, moved by his despair, had bought and freed and given her back to him, with the promise that she never should be torn from him again. For an instant the clasp of little clinging arms seemed to make the sore chafing of the iron ring unfelt; the touch of the hand that gave the precious gift now made that rude weapon weigh heavily in his own, and from the darkness which lay between him and the doomed home there seemed to rise the shadow of the face which once had looked compassionately into his and recognized him as a man. He turned, and, standing with his magnificent yet mournful figure fully revealed by the red flicker of the torches, put out one hand as if to withhold the desperate crowd before him, and asked, with an air of authority which well became a prince by birth as well as name,—

"Sandra, who tole you massa meant ter free us right away? You has blessed dreams sometimes, and maybe dis is one ob 'em. It's too good to be de troof."

"It is de troof, de livin' troof, and no dream ob mine was eber half so blessed as dis yere will be, if we has faith. Milly tole me jes now dat Massa Gabriel swore before de Lord and his dead father dat he'd free us all ter-morrer; and I come here ter save yer from de sin dat won't help, but hinder yer awful in dis world and de next. Dere's more good news 'sides dat. I heerd 'em talkin' 'bout de Norf. It's risin', boys, it's risin'!—de tings we's heerd is shore, and de day ob jubilee is comin' fas'."

It was well she added that last hope, for its effect was wonderful. Men lifted up their heads, hope quenched hatred in eyes that grew joyfully expectant, and for a moment the black sky seemed to glimmer with the first rays of the North star which should lead them up from that Dismal Swamp to a goodly land. Sandra felt the change, knew that only one more effective touch was needed to secure the victory, and, like the pious soul she was, turned in her hour of need to the only Friend who never had deserted her. Painfully bending her stiff knees, she knelt down before them, folded her hard hands, lifted her sightless eyes, and cried, in an agony of supplication,—

"Dear Lord, speak to dese yere pore chil'en, for I'se done my bes'! Help 'em, save 'em, don't let 'em spile de freedom dat's comin' by a sin like dis to-night, but let 'em take it sweet and clean from Thy han' in de mornin'. Stan' by young massa, hole him up, don't let him 'spoint us, fer we'se been bery patient, Lord; and help us to wait one night more, shore dat he'll keep de promise for Thy blessed sake."

"I will!"

The voice rang through the place like a voice from heaven; and out from the darkness Gabriel came among them. To their startled, supersti-tious eyes he seemed no mortal man, but a beautiful, benignant angel, bringing tidings of great joy, as he stood there, armed with no weapon but a righteous purpose, gifted with no eloquence but the truth, stirred to his heart's core by strong emotion, and lifted above himself by the high mood born of that memorable hour.

"My people! mine only while I speak; break up your league, lay down your arms, dry your tears, and forgive as you are forgiven, for this island no longer holds a master or a slave; but all are free forever and forever."

An awful silence fell upon the place, unbroken till old Sandra cried, with a glad, triumphant voice,—

"Chil'en! de Lord hab heerd, de Lord hab answered! Bless de Lord! O bless de Lord!"

Then, as a strong wind bows a field of grain, the breath of liberty swept over fifty souls, and down upon their knees fell fifty free men, while a great cry went up to heaven. Shouts, sobs, prayers and praises; the clash of falling arms; the rattle of fetters wrenched away; the rush of men gathered to each other's breasts,—all added to the wild abandonment of a happiness too mighty for adequate expression, as that wave of gratitude and love rolled up and broke at Gabriel's feet. With face hidden in his hands he stood; and while his heart sung for joy, tears from the deepest fountains of a man's repentant spirit fitly baptized the freedmen, who, clinging to his garments, kissing his feet and pouring blessings on his head, bestowed upon him a far nobler inheritance than that which he had lost.

"Hark!"

The word, and Sandra's uplifted hand, hushed the tumultuous thanksgiving, as if she were in truth the magician they believed her. A far-off murmur of many voices, the tramp of many feet was heard; all knew what it portended, yet none trembled, none fled; for a mightier power than either force or fear had conquered, and the victory was already won.

Through widening rifts in the stormy sky the moon broke clear and calm, gliding, like a visible benediction, from the young man's bent head to the dusky faces lifted toward the promised light; and in that momentary hush, solemn and sweet, across the river a distant clock struck twelve.

MY CONTRABAND

*D*OCTOR FRANCK came in as I sat sewing up the rents in an old shirt, that Tom might go tidily to his grave. New shirts were needed for the living, and there was no wife or mother to "dress him handsome when he went to meet the Lord," as one woman said, describing the fine funeral she had pinched herself to give her son.

"Miss Dane, I'm in a quandary," began the Doctor, with that expression of countenance which says as plainly as words, "I want to ask a favor, but I wish you'd save me the trouble."

"Can I help you out of it?"

"Faith! I don't like to propose it, but you certainly can, if you please."

"Then name it, I beg."

"You see a Reb has just been brought in crazy with typhoid; a bad case every way; a drunken, rascally little captain somebody took the trouble to capture, but whom nobody wants to take the trouble to cure. The wards are full, the ladies worked to death, and willing to be for our own boys, but rather slow to risk their lives for a Reb. Now, you've had the fever, you like queer patients, your mate will see to your ward for a while, and I will find you a good attendant. The fellow won't last long, I fancy; but he can't die without some sort of care, you know. I've put him in the fourth story of the west wing, away from the rest. It is airy, quiet, and comfortable there. I'm on that ward, and will do my best for you in every way. Now, then, will you go?"

"Of course I will, out of perversity, if not common charity; for some of these people think that because I'm an abolitionist I am also a heathen, and I should rather like to show them that, though I cannot quite love my enemies, I am willing to take care of them."

"Very good; I thought you'd go; and speaking of abolition reminds me that you can have a contraband for servant, if you like. It is that fine mu-

First published as "The Brothers" in the *Atlantic Monthly* 12, no. 73 (November 1863). Reprinted in *Hospital Sketches and Camp and Fireside Stories,* 1869.

latto fellow who was found burying his rebel master after the fight, and, being badly cut over the head, our boys brought him along. Will you have him?"

"By all means,—for I'll stand to my guns on that point, as on the other; these black boys are far more faithful and handy than some of the white scamps given me to serve, instead of being served by. But is this man well enough?"

"Yes, for that sort of work, and I think you'll like him. He must have been a handsome fellow before he got his face slashed; not much darker than myself; his master's son, I dare say, and the white blood makes him rather high and haughty about some things. He was in a bad way when he came in, but vowed he'd die in the street rather than turn in with the black fellows below; so I put him up in the west wing, to be out of the way, and he's seen to the captain all the morning. When can you go up?"

"As soon as Tom is laid out, Skinner moved, Haywood washed, Marble dressed, Charley rubbed, Downs taken up, Upham laid down, and the whole forty fed."

We both laughed, though the Doctor was on his way to the dead-house and I held a shroud on my lap. But in a hospital one learns that cheerfulness is one's salvation; for, in an atmosphere of suffering and death, heaviness of heart would soon paralyze usefulness of hand, if the blessed gift of smiles had been denied us.

In an hour I took possession of my new charge, finding a dissipated-looking boy of nineteen or twenty raving in the solitary little room, with no one near him but the contraband in the room adjoining. Feeling decidedly more interest in the black man than in the white, yet remembering the Doctor's hint of his being "high and haughty," I glanced furtively at him as I scattered chloride of lime about the room to purify the air, and settled matters to suit myself. I had seen many contrabands, but never one so attractive as this. All colored men are called "boys," even if their heads are white; this boy was five-and-twenty at least, strong-limbed and manly, and had the look of one who never had been cowed by abuse or worn with oppressive labor. He sat on his bed doing nothing; no book, no pipe, no pen or paper anywhere appeared, yet anything less indolent or listless than his attitude and expression I never saw. Erect he sat, with a hand on either knee, and eyes fixed on the bare wall opposite, so rapt in some absorbing thought as to be unconscious of my presence, though the door stood wide open and my movements were by no means noiseless. His face was half averted, but I instantly approved the Doctor's taste, for the profile which I saw possessed all the attributes of comeliness belonging to his mixed race. He was more quadroon than mulatto, with Saxon features, Spanish complexion darkened by exposure, color in lips and cheek, waving hair, and an eye full of the passionate melancholy which in such men always seems to utter a mute protest against the broken law that doomed them at their birth. What could he be thinking of? The sick boy cursed and raved, I rustled to and fro, steps passed the door, bells rang, and the steady rumble of army-wagons came up from the street, still he never stirred. I had seen colored people in what they call "the black sulks," when, for days, they neither smiled nor spoke, and scarcely ate. But this was something more than that; for the man was not dully brooding over some small grievance; he seemed to see an all-absorbing fact or fancy recorded on the wall, which was a blank to me. I wondered if it were some deep wrong or sorrow, kept alive by memory and impotent regret; if he mourned for the dead master to whom he had been faithful to the end; or if the liberty now his were robbed of half its sweetness by the knowledge that some one near and dear to him still languished in the hell from which he had escaped. My heart quite warmed to him at that idea; I wanted to know and comfort him; and, following the impulse of the moment, I went in and touched him on the shoulder.

In an instant the man vanished and the slave appeared. Freedom was too new a boon to have wrought its blessed changes yet; and as he started up, with his hand at his temple, and an obsequious "Yes, Missis," any romance that had gathered round him fled away, leaving the saddest of all sad facts in living guise before me. Not only did the manhood seem to die out of him, but the comeliness that first attracted me; for, as he turned, I saw the ghastly wound that had laid open cheek and forehead. Being partly healed, it was no longer bandaged, but held together with strips of that transparent plaster which I never see without a shiver, and swift recollections of the scenes with which it is associated in my mind. Part of his black hair had been shorn away, and one eye was nearly closed; pain so distorted, and the cruel sabre-cut so marred that portion of his face, that, when I saw it, I felt as if a fine medal had been suddenly reversed, showing me a far more striking type of human suffering and wrong than Michael Angelo's bronze prisoner. By one of those inexplicable processes that often teach us how little we understand ourselves, my purpose was suddenly changed; and, though I went in to offer comfort as a friend, I merely gave an order as a mistress.

"Will you open these windows? this man needs more air."

He obeyed at once, and, as he slowly urged up the unruly sash, the handsome profile was again turned toward me, and again I was possessed by my first impression so strongly that I involuntarily said,—

"Thank you."

Perhaps it was fancy, but I thought that in the look of mingled surprise and something like reproach which he gave me, there was also a trace of grateful pleasure. But he said, in that tone of spiritless humility these poor souls learn so soon,—

"I isn't a white man, Missis, I'se a contraband."

"Yes, I know it; but a contraband is a free man, and I heartily congratulate you."

He liked that; his face shone, he squared his shoulders, lifted his head, and looked me full in the eye with a brisk,—

"Thank ye, Missis; anything more to do fer yer?"

"Doctor Franck thought you would help me with this man, as there are many patients and few nurses or attendants. Have you had the fever?"

"No, Missis."

"They should have thought of that when they put him here; wounds and fevers should not be together. I'll try to get you moved."

He laughed a sudden laugh: if he had been a white man, I should have called it scornful; as he was a few shades darker than myself, I suppose it must be considered an insolent, or at least an unmannerly one.

"It don't matter, Missis. I'd rather be up here with the fever than down with those niggers; and there isn't no other place fer me."

Poor fellow! that was true. No ward in all the hospital would take him in to lie side by side with the most miserable white wreck there. Like the bat in Æsop's fable, he belonged to neither race; and the pride of one and the helplessness of the other, kept him hovering alone in the twilight a great sin has brought to over-shadow the whole land.

"You shall stay, then; for I would far rather have you than my lazy Jack. But are you well and strong enough?"

"I guess I'll do, Missis."

He spoke with a passive sort of acquiescence,—as if it did not much matter if he were not able, and no one would particularly rejoice if he were.

"Yes, I think you will. By what name shall I call you?"

"Bob, Missis."

Every woman has her pet whim; one of mine was to teach the men self-respect by treating them respectfully. Tom, Dick, and Harry would pass, when lads rejoiced in those familiar abbreviations; but to address men often old enough to be my father in that style did not suit my old-fashioned ideas of propriety. This "Bob" would never die; I should have found it as easy to call the chaplain "Gus" as my tragical-looking contraband by a title so strongly associated with the tail of a kite.

"What is your other name?" I asked. "I like to call my attendants by their last names rather than by their first."

"I'se got no other, Missis; we has our master's names, or do without. Mine's dead, and I won't have anything of his 'bout me."

"Well, I'll call you Robert, then, and you may fill this pitcher for me, if you will be so kind."

He went; but, through all the tame obedience years of servitude had taught him, I could see that the proud spirit his father gave him was not yet subdued, for the look and gesture with which he repudiated his master's name were a more effective declaration of independence than any Fourth-of-July orator could have prepared.

We spent a curious week together. Robert seldom left his room, except upon my errands; and I was a prisoner all day, often all night, by the bedside of the rebel. The fever burned itself rapidly away, for there seemed little vitality to feed it in the feeble frame of this old young man, whose life had been none of the most righteous, judging from the revelations made by his unconscious lips; since more than once Robert authoritatively silenced him, when my gentler hushings were of no avail, and blasphemous wanderings or ribald camp-songs made my cheeks burn and Robert's face assume an aspect of disgust. The captain was a gentleman in the world's eye, but the contraband was the gentleman in mine;—I was a fanatic, and that accounts for such depravity of taste, I hope. I never asked Robert of himself, feeling that somewhere there was a spot still too sore to bear the lightest touch; but, from his language, manner, and intelligence, I inferred that his color had procured for him the few advantages within the reach of a quick-witted, kindly-treated slave. Silent, grave, and thoughtful, but most serviceable, was my contraband; glad of the books I brought him, faithful in the performance of the duties I assigned to him, grateful for the friendliness I could not but feel and show toward him. Often I longed to ask what purpose was so visibly altering his aspect with such daily deepening gloom. But I never dared, and no one else had either time or desire to pry into the past of this specimen of one branch of the chivalrous "F. F. Vs."

On the seventh night, Dr. Franck suggested that it would be well for some one, besides the general watchman of the ward, to be with the captain, as it might be his last. Although the greater part of the two preceding nights had been spent there, of course I offered to remain,—for there is a strange fascination in these scenes, which renders one careless of fatigue and unconscious of fear until the crisis is past.

"Give him water as long as he can drink, and if he drops into a natural sleep, it may save him. I'll look in at midnight, when some change will probably take place. Nothing but sleep or a miracle will keep him now. Good-night."

Away went the Doctor; and, devouring a whole mouthful of grapes, I lowered the lamp, wet the captain's head, and sat down on a hard stool to begin my watch. The captain lay with his hot, haggard face turned toward me, filling the air with his poisonous breath, and feebly muttering, with lips and tongue so parched that the sanest speech would have been difficult to understand. Robert was stretched on his bed in the inner room, the door of which stood ajar, that a fresh draught from his open window might carry the fever-fumes away through mine. I could just see a long, dark figure, with the lighter outline of a face, and, having little else to do just then, I fell to thinking of this curious contraband, who evidently prized his freedom highly, yet seemed in no haste to enjoy it. Dr. Franck had offered to send him on to safer quarters, but he had said, "No, thank yer, sir, not yet," and then had gone away to fall into one of those black moods of his, which began to disturb me, because I had no power to lighten them. As I sat listening to the clocks from the steeples all about us, I amused myself with planning Robert's future, as I often did my own, and had dealt out to him a generous hand of trumps wherewith to play this game of life which hitherto had gone so cruelly against him, when a harsh choked voice called,—

"Lucy!"

It was the captain, and some new terror seemed to have gifted him with momentary strength.

"Yes, here's Lucy," I answered, hoping that by following the fancy I might quiet him,—for his face was damp with the clammy moisture, and his frame shaken with the nervous tremor that so often precedes death. His dull eye fixed upon me, dilating with a bewildered look of incredulity and wrath, till he broke out fiercely,—

"That's a lie! she's dead,—and so's Bob, damn him!"

Finding speech a failure, I began to sing the quiet tune that had often soothed delirium like this; but hardly had the line,—

"See gentle patience smile on pain,"

passed my lips, when he clutched me by the wrist, whispering like one in mortal fear,—

"Hush! she used to sing that way to Bob, but she never would to me. I swore I'd whip the devil out of her, and I did; but you know before she cut her throat she said she'd haunt me, and there she is!"

He pointed behind me with an aspect of such pale dismay, that I involuntarily glanced over my shoulder and started as if I had seen a veritable ghost; for, peering from the gloom of that inner room, I saw a shadowy face, with dark hair all about it, and a glimpse of scarlet at the throat. An instant showed me that it was only Robert leaning from his bed's foot, wrapped in a gray army-blanket, with his red shirt just visible above it, and his long hair disordered by sleep. But what a strange expression was on his face! The unmarred side was toward me, fixed and motionless as when I first observed it,—less absorbed now, but more intent. His eye glittered, his lips were apart like one who listened with every sense, and his whole aspect reminded me of a hound to which some wind had brought the scent of unsuspected prey.

"Do you know him, Robert? Does he mean you?"

"Laws, no, Missis; they all own half-a-dozen Bobs: but hearin' my name woke me; that's all."

He spoke quite naturally, and lay down again, while I returned to my charge, thinking that this paroxysm was probably his last. But by another hour I perceived a hopeful change; for the tremor had subsided, the cold dew was gone, his breathing was more regular, and Sleep, the healer, had descended to save or take him gently away. Doctor Franck looked in at midnight, bade me keep all cool and quiet, and not fail to administer a certain draught as soon as the captain woke. Very much relieved, I laid my head on my arms, uncomfortably folded on the little table, and fancied I was about to perform one of the feats which practice renders possible,— "sleeping with one eye open," as we say: a half-and-half doze, for all senses sleep but that of hearing; the faintest murmur, sigh, or motion will break it, and give one back one's wits much brightened by the brief permission to "stand at ease." On this night the experiment was a failure, for previous vigils, confinement, and much care had rendered naps a dangerous indulgence. Having roused half-a-dozen times in an hour to find all quiet, I dropped my heavy head on my arms, and, drowsily resolving to look up again in fifteen minutes, fell fast asleep.

The striking of a deep-voiced clock awoke me with a start. "That is one," thought I; but, to my dismay, two more strokes followed, and in remorseful haste I sprang up to see what harm my long oblivion had done. A strong hand put me back into my seat, and held me there. It was Robert. The instant my eye met his my heart began to beat, and all along my nerves tingled that electric flash which foretells a danger that we cannot see. He was very pale, his mouth grim, and both eyes full of sombre fire; for even the wounded one was open now, all the more sinister for the deep scar above and below. But his touch was steady, his voice quiet, as he said,—

"Sit still, Missis; I won't hurt yer, nor scare yer, ef I can help it, but yer waked too soon."

"Let me go, Robert,—the captain is stirring,—I must give him something."

"No, Missis, yer can't stir an inch. Look here!"

Holding me with one hand, with the other he took up the glass in which I had left the draught, and showed me it was empty.

"Has he taken it?" I asked, more and more bewildered.

"I flung it out o' winder, Missis; he'll have to do without."

"But why, Robert? why did you do it?"

"'Kase I hate him!"

Impossible to doubt the truth of that; his whole face showed it, as he spoke through his set teeth, and launched a fiery glance at the unconscious captain. I could only hold my breath and stare blankly at him, wondering what mad act was coming next. I suppose I shook and turned white, as women have a foolish habit of doing when sudden danger daunts them; for Robert released my arm, sat down upon the bedside just in front of me, and said, with the ominous quietude that made me cold to see and hear,—

"Don't yer be frightened, Missis; don't try to run away, fer the door's locked and the key in my pocket; don't yer cry out, fer yer'd have to scream a long while, with my hand on yer mouth, 'efore yer was heard. Be still, an' I'll tell yer what I'm gwine to do."

"Lord help us! he has taken the fever in some sudden, violent way, and is out of his head. I must humor him till some one comes"; in pursuance of which swift determination, I tried to say, quite composedly,—

"I will be still and hear you; but open the window. Why did you shut it?"

"I'm sorry I can't do it, Missis; but yer'd jump out, or call, if I did, an' I'm not ready yet. I shut it to make yer sleep, an' heat would do it quicker'n anything else I could do."

The captain moved, and feebly muttered "Water!" Instinctively I rose to give it to him, but the heavy hand came down upon my shoulder, and in the same decided tone Robert said,—

"The water went with the physic; let him call."

"Do let me go to him! he'll die without care!"

"I mean he shall;—don't yer meddle, if yer please, Missis."

In spite of his quiet tone and respectful manner, I saw murder in his eyes, and turned faint with fear; yet the fear excited me, and, hardly knowing what I did, I seized the hands that had seized me, crying,—

"No, no; you shall not kill him! It is base to hurt a helpless man. Why do you hate him? He is not your master."

"He's my brother."

I felt that answer from head to foot, and seemed to fathom what was coming, with a prescience vague, but unmistakable. One appeal was left to me, and I made it.

"Robert, tell me what it means? Do not commit a crime and make me accessory to it. There is a better way of righting wrong than by violence;—let me help you find it."

My voice trembled as I spoke, and I heard the frightened flutter of my heart; so did he, and if any little act of mine had ever won affection or respect from him, the memory of it served me then. He looked down, and seemed to put some question to himself; whatever it was, the answer was in my favor, for when his eyes rose again, they were gloomy, but not desperate.

"I *will* tell yer, Missis; but mind, this makes no difference; the boy is mine. I'll give the Lord a chance to take him fust: if He don't, I shall."

"Oh, no! remember he is your brother."

An unwise speech; I felt it as it passed my lips, for a black frown gathered on Robert's face, and his strong hands closed with an ugly sort of grip. But he did not touch the poor soul gasping there behind him, and seemed content to let the slow suffocation of that stifling room end his frail life.

"I'm not like to forgit dat, Missis, when I've been thinkin' of it all this week. I knew him when they fetched him in, an' would 'a' done it long 'fore this, but I wanted to ask where Lucy was; he knows,—he told to-night,—an' now he's done for."

"Who is Lucy?" I asked hurriedly, intent on keeping his mind busy with any thought but murder.

With one of the swift transitions of a mixed temperament like this, at my question Robert's deep eyes filled, the clenched hands were spread before his face, and all I heard were the broken words,—

"My wife,—he took her——"

In that instant every thought of fear was swallowed up in burning indignation for the wrong, and a perfect passion of pity for the desperate man so tempted to avenge an injury for which there seemed no redress but this. He was no longer slave or contraband, no drop of black blood marred him in my sight, but an infinite compassion yearned to save, to help, to comfort him. Words seemed so powerless I offered none, only put my hand on his poor head, wounded, homeless, bowed down with grief for which I had no cure, and softly smoothed the long, neglected hair, pitifully wondering the while where was the wife who must have loved this tender-hearted man so well.

The captain moaned again, and faintly whispered, "Air!" but I never stirred. God forgive me! just then I hated him only as a woman thinking of a sister woman's wrong could hate. Robert looked up; his eyes were dry again, his mouth grim. I saw that, said, "Tell me more," and he did; for sympathy is a gift the poorest may give, the proudest stoop to receive.

"Yer see, Missis, his father,—I might say ours, ef I warn't ashamed of both of 'em,—his father died two years ago, an' left us all to Marster Ned,—that's him here, eighteen then. He always hated me, I looked so like old Marster: he don't,—only the light skin an' hair. Old Marster was kind to all of us, me 'specially, an' bought Lucy off the next plantation down there in South Car'lina, when he found I liked her. I married her, all I could; it warn't much, but we was true to one another till Marster Ned come home a year after an' made hell fer both of us. He sent my old mother to be used up in his rice-swamp in Georgy; he found me with my pretty Lucy, an' though young Miss cried, an' I prayed to him on my knees, an' Lucy run away, he wouldn't have no mercy; he brought her back, an'—took her."

"Oh, what did you do?" I cried, hot with helpless pain and passion.

How the man's outraged heart sent the blood flaming up into his face and deepened the tones of his impetuous voice, as he stretched his arm across the bed, saying, with a terribly expressive gesture,—

"I half murdered him, an' to-night I'll finish."

"Yes, yes,—but go on now; what came next?"

He gave me a look that showed no white man could have felt a deeper degradation in remembering and confessing these last acts of brotherly oppression.

"They whipped me till I couldn't stand, an' then they sold me further South. Yer thought I was a white man once,—look here!"

With a sudden wrench he tore the shirt from neck to waist, and on his strong, brown shoulders showed me furrows deeply ploughed, wounds which, though healed, were ghastlier to me than any in that house. I could not speak to him, and, with the pathetic dignity a great grief lends the humblest sufferer, he ended his brief tragedy by simply saying,—

"That's all, Missis. I'se never seen her since, an' now I never shall in this world,—maybe not in t'other."

"But, Robert, why think her dead? The captain was wandering when he said those sad things; perhaps he will retract them when he is sane. Don't despair; don't give up yet."

"No, Missis, I'spect he's right; she was too proud to bear that long. It's like her to kill herself. I told her to, if there was no other way; an' she always minded me, Lucy did. My poor girl! Oh, it warn't right! No, by God, it warn't!"

As the memory of this bitter wrong, this double bereavement, burned in his sore heart, the devil that lurks in every strong man's blood leaped up; he put his hand upon his brother's throat, and, watching the white face before him, muttered low between his teeth,—

"I'm lettin' him go too easy; there's no pain in this; we a'n't even yet. I wish he knew me. Marster Ned! it's Bob; where's Lucy?"

From the captain's lips there came a long faint sigh, and nothing but a flutter of the eyelids showed that he still lived. A strange stillness filled the room as the elder brother held the younger's life suspended in his hand, while wavering between a dim hope and a deadly hate. In the whirl of thoughts that went on in my brain, only one was clear enough to act upon. I must prevent murder, if I could,—but how? What could I do up there alone, locked in with a dying man and a lunatic?—for any mind yielded utterly to any unrighteous impulse is mad while the impulse rules it. Strength I had not, nor much courage, neither time nor wit for stratagem, and chance only could bring me help before it was too late. But one weapon I possessed,—a tongue,—often a woman's best defence; and sympathy, stronger than fear, gave me power to use it. What I said Heaven only knows, but surely Heaven helped me; words burned on my lips, tears streamed from my eyes, and some good angel prompted me to use the one name that had power to arrest my hearer's hand and touch his heart. For at that moment I heartily believed that Lucy lived, and this earnest faith roused in him a like belief.

He listened with the lowering look of one in whom brute instinct was sovereign for the time,—a look that makes the noblest countenance base. He was but a man,—a poor, untaught, outcast, outraged man. Life had few joys for him; the world offered him no honors, no success, no home, no love. What future would this crime mar? and why should he deny himself that sweet, yet bitter morsel called revenge? How many white men, with all New England's freedom, culture, Christianity, would not have felt as he felt then? Should I have reproached him for a human anguish, a human longing for redress, all now left him from the ruin of his few poor hopes? Who had taught him that self-control, self-sacrifice, are attributes that make men masters of the earth, and lift them nearer heaven? Should I have urged the beauty of forgiveness, the duty of devout submission? He had no religion, for he was no saintly "Uncle Tom," and Slavery's black shadow seemed to darken all the world to him, and shut out God. Should I have warned him of penalties, of judgments, and the potency of law? What did he know of justice, or the mercy that should temper that stern virtue, when every law, human and divine, had been broken on his hearthstone? Should I have tried to touch him by appeals to filial duty, to brotherly love? How had his appeals been answered? What memories had father and brother stored up in his heart to plead for either now? No,—all those influences, those associations, would have proved worse than useless, had I been calm enough to try them. I was not; but instinct, subtler than reason, showed me the one safe clue by which to lead this troubled soul from the labyrinth in which it groped and nearly fell. When I paused, breathless, Robert turned to me, asking, as if human assurances could strengthen his faith in Divine Omnipotence,—

"Do you believe, if I let Marster Ned live, the Lord will give me back my Lucy?"

"As surely as there is a Lord, you will find her here or in the beautiful hereafter, where there is no black or white, no master and no slave."

He took his hand from his brother's throat, lifted his eyes from my face to the wintry sky beyond, as if searching for that blessed country, happier even than the happy North. Alas, it was the darkest hour before the dawn!—there was no star above, no light below but the pale glimmer of the lamp that showed the brother who had made him desolate. Like a blind man who believes there is a sun, yet cannot see it, he shook his head, let his arms drop nervelessly upon his knees, and sat there dumbly asking that question which many a soul whose faith is firmer fixed than his has asked in hours less dark than this,—"Where is God?" I saw the tide had turned, and strenuously tried to keep this rudderless life-boat from slipping back into the whirlpool wherein it had been so nearly lost.

"I have listened to you, Robert; now hear me, and heed what I say, because my heart is full of pity for you, full of hope for your future, and a desire to help you now. I want you to go away from here, from the temptation of this place, and the sad thoughts that haunt it. You have conquered yourself once, and I honor you for it, because, the harder the battle, the more glorious the victory; but it is safer to put a greater distance between you and this man. I will write you letters, give you money, and send you to good old Massachusetts to begin your new life a freeman,—yes, and a happy man; for when the captain is himself again, I will learn where Lucy is, and move heaven and earth to find and give her back to you. Will you do this, Robert?"

Slowly, very slowly, the answer came; for the purpose of a week, perhaps a year, was hard to relinquish in an hour.

"Yes, Missis, I will."

"Good! Now you are the man I thought you, and I'll work for you with all my heart. You need sleep, my poor fellow; go, and try to forget. The captain is alive, and as yet you are spared that sin. No, don't look there; I'll care for him. Come, Robert, for Lucy's sake."

Thank Heaven for the immortality of love! for when all other means of salvation failed, a spark of this vital fire softened the man's iron will, until a woman's hand could bend it. He let me take from him the key, let me draw him gently away, and lead him to the solitude which now was the most healing balm I could bestow. Once in his little room, he fell down on his bed and lay there, as if spent with the sharpest conflict of his life. I slipped the bolt across his door, and unlocked my own, flung up the window, steadied myself with a breath of air, then rushed to Doctor Franck. He came; and till dawn we worked together, saving one brother's life, and taking earnest thought how best to secure the other's liberty. When the sun came up as blithely as if it shone only upon happy homes, the Doctor went to Robert. For an hour I heard the murmur of their voices; once I caught the sound of heavy sobs, and for a time a reverent hush, as if in the silence that good man were ministering to soul as well as body. When he departed he took Robert with him, pausing to tell me he should get him off as soon as possible, but not before we met again.

Nothing more was seen of them all day; another surgeon came to see the captain, and another attendant came to fill the empty place. I tried to rest, but could not, with the thought of poor Lucy tugging at my heart, and was soon back at my post again, anxiously hoping that my contraband had not been too hastily spirited away. Just as night fell there came a tap, and, opening, I saw Robert literally "clothed, and in his right mind." The Doctor had replaced the ragged suit with tidy garments, and no trace of that tempestuous night remained but deeper lines upon the forehead, and the docile look of a repentant child. He did not cross the threshold, did not offer me his hand,—only took off his cap, saying, with a traitorous falter in his voice,—

"God bless yer, Missis! I'm gwine."

I put out both my hands, and held his fast.

"Good-by, Robert! Keep up good heart, and when I come home to Massachusetts we'll meet in a happier place than this. Are you quite ready, quite comfortable for your journey?"

"Yes, Missis, yes; the Doctor's fixed everything; I'se gwine with a friend of his; my papers are all right, an' I'm as happy as I can be till I find"——

He stopped there; then went on, with a glance into the room,—

"I'm glad I didn't do it, an' I thank yer, Missis, fer hinderin' me,—thank yer hearty; but I'm afraid I hate him jest the same."

Of course he did; and so did I; for these faulty hearts of ours cannot turn perfect in a night, but need frost and fire, wind and rain, to ripen and make them ready for the great harvest-home. Wishing to divert his mind, I put my poor mite into his hand, and, remembering the magic of a certain little book, I gave him mine, on whose dark cover whitely shone the Virgin Mother and the Child, the grand history of whose life the book contained. The money went into Robert's pocket with a grateful murmur, the book into his bosom, with a long look and a tremulous—

"I never saw *my* baby, Missis."

I broke down then; and though my eyes were too dim to see, I felt the touch of lips upon my hands, heard the sound of departing feet, and knew my contraband was gone.

When one feels an intense dislike, the less one says about the subject of it the better; therefore I shall merely record that the captain lived,—in time was exchanged; and that, whoever the other party was, I am convinced the Government got the best of the bargain. But long before this occurred, I had fulfilled my promise to Robert; for as soon as my patient recovered strength of memory enough to make his answer trustworthy, I asked, without any circumlocution,—

"Captain Fairfax, where is Lucy?"

And too feeble to be angry, surprised, or insincere, he straightway answered,—

"Dead, Miss Dane."

"And she killed herself when you sold Bob?"

"How the devil did you know that?" he muttered, with an expression half-remorseful, half-amazed; but I was satisfied, and said no more.

Of course this went to Robert, waiting far away there in a lonely home,—waiting, working, hoping for his Lucy. It almost broke my heart to do it; but delay was weak, deceit was wicked; so I sent the heavy tidings, and very soon the answer came,—only three lines; but I felt that the sustaining power of the man's life was gone.

"I tort I'd never see her any more; I'm glad to know she's out of trouble.

I thank yer, Missis; an' if they let us, I'll fight fer yer till I'm killed, which I hope will be 'fore long."

Six months later he had his wish, and kept his word.

Every one knows the story of the attack on Fort Wagner; but we should not tire yet of recalling how our Fifty-Fourth, spent with three sleepless nights, a day's fast, and a march under the July sun, stormed the fort as night fell, facing death in many shapes, following their brave leaders through a fiery rain of shot and shell, fighting valiantly for "God and Governor Andrew,"—how the regiment that went into action seven hundred strong, came out having had nearly half its number captured, killed, or wounded, leaving their young commander to be buried, like a chief of earlier times, with his body-guard around him, faithful to the death. Surely, the insult turns to honor, and the wide grave needs no monument but the heroism that consecrates it in our sight; surely, the hearts that held him nearest, see through their tears a noble victory in the seeming sad defeat; and surely, God's benediction was bestowed, when this loyal soul answered, as Death called the roll, "Lord, here am I, with the brothers Thou hast given me!"

The future must show how well that fight was fought; for though Fort Wagner once defied us, public prejudice is down; and through the cannon-smoke of that black night, the manhood of the colored race shines before many eyes that would not see, rings in many ears that would not hear, wins many hearts that would not hitherto believe.

When the news came that we were needed, there was none so glad as I to leave teaching contrabands, the new work I had taken up, and go to nurse "our boys," as my dusky flock so proudly called the wounded of the Fifty-Fourth. Feeling more satisfaction, as I assumed my big apron and turned up my cuffs, than if dressing for the President's levee, I fell to work in Hospital No. 10 at Beaufort. The scene was most familiar, and yet strange; for only dark faces looked up at me from the pallets so thickly laid along the floor, and I missed the sharp accent of my Yankee boys in the slower, softer voices calling cheerily to one another, or answering my questions with a stout, "We'll never give it up, Missis, till the last Reb's dead," or, "If our people's free, we can afford to die."

Passing from bed to bed, intent on making one pair of hands do the work of three, at least, I gradually washed, fed, and bandaged my way down the long line of sable heroes, and coming to the very last, found that he was my contraband. So old, so worn, so deathly weak and wan, I never should have known him but for the deep scar on his cheek. That side lay uppermost, and caught my eye at once; but even then I doubted, such an awful change had come upon him, when, turning to the ticket just above his head, I saw the name, "Robert Dane." That both assured and touched me, for, remembering that he had no name, I knew that he had taken mine. I longed for him to speak to me, to tell how he had fared since I lost sight of him, and let me perform some little service for him in return for many he had done for me; but he seemed asleep; and as I stood re-living that strange night again, a bright lad, who lay next him softly waving an old fan across both beds, looked up and said,—

"I guess you know him, Missis?"

"You are right. Do you?"

"As much as any one was able to, Missis."

"Why do you say 'was,' as if the man were dead and gone?"

"I s'pose because I know he'll have to go. He's got a bad jab in the breast, an' is bleedin' inside, the Doctor says. He don't suffer any, only gets weaker 'n' weaker every minute. I've been fannin' him this long while, an' he's talked a little; but he don't know me now, so he's most gone, I guess."

There was so much sorrow and affection in the boy's face, that I remembered something, and asked, with redoubled interest,—

"Are you the one that brought him off? I was told about a boy who nearly lost his life in saving that of his mate."

I dare say the young fellow blushed, as any modest lad might have done; I could not see it, but I heard the chuckle of satisfaction that escaped him, as he glanced from his shattered arm and bandaged side to the pale figure opposite.

"Lord, Missis, that's nothin'; we boys always stan' by one another, an' I warn't goin' to leave him to be tormented any more by them cussed Rebs. He's been a slave once, though he don't look half so much like it as me, an' I was born in Boston."

He did not; for the speaker was as black as the ace of spades,—being a sturdy specimen, the knave of clubs would perhaps be a fitter representative,—but the dark freeman looked at the white slave with the pitiful, yet puzzled expression I have so often seen on the faces of our wisest men, when his tangled question of Slavery presented itself, asking to be cut or patiently undone.

"Tell me what you know of this man; for, even if he were awake, he is too weak to talk."

"I never saw him till I joined the regiment, an' no one 'peared to have got much out of him. He was a shut-up sort of feller, an' didn't seem to care for anything but gettin' at the Rebs. Some say he was the fust man of us that enlisted; I know he fretted till we were off, an' when we pitched into old Wagner, he fought like the devil."

"Were you with him when he was wounded? How was it?"

"Yes, Missis. There was somethin' queer about it; for he 'peared to know the chap that killed him, an' the chap knew him. I don't dare to ask, t rather guess one owned the other some time; for, when they clinched, t..e chap sung out, 'Bob!' an' Dane, 'Marster Ned!'—then they went at it."

I sat down suddenly, for the old anger and compassion struggled in my heart, and I both longed and feared to hear what was to follow.

"You see, when the Colonel,—Lord keep an' send him back to us!—it a'n't certain yet, you know, Missis, though it's two days ago we lost him,— well, when the Colonel shouted, 'Rush on, boys, rush on!' Dane tore away as if he was goin' to take the fort alone; I was next him, an' kept close as we went through the ditch an' up the wall. Hi! warn't that a rusher!" and the boy flung up his well arm with a whoop, as if the mere memory of that stirring moment came over him in a gust of irrepressible excitement.

"Were you afraid?" I said, asking the question women often put, and receiving the answer they seldom fail to get.

"No, Missis!"—emphasis on the "Missis"—"I never thought of any-thing but the damn' Rebs, that scalp, slash, an' cut our ears off, when they git us. I was bound to let daylight into one of 'em at least, an' I did. Hope he liked it!"

"It is evident that you did. Now go on about Robert, for I should be at work."

"He was one of the fust up; I was just behind, an' though the whole thing happened in a minute, I remember how it was, for all I was yellin' an' knockin' round like mad. Just where we were, some sort of an officer was wavin' his sword an' cheerin' on his men; Dane saw him by a big flash that come by; he flung away his gun, give a leap, an' went at that feller as if he was Jeff, Beauregard, an' Lee, all in one. I scrabbled after as quick as I could, but was only up in time to see him git the sword straight through him an' drop into the ditch. You needn't ask what I did next, Missis, for I don't quite know myself; all I'm clear about is, that I managed somehow to pitch that Reb into the fort as dead as Moses, git hold of Dane, an' bring him off. Poor old feller! we said we went in to live or die; he said he went in to die, an' he's done it."

I had been intently watching the excited speaker; but as he regretfully added those last words I turned again, and Robert's eyes met mine,—those melancholy eyes, so full of an intelligence that proved he had heard, re-membered, and reflected with that preternatural power which often outlives all other faculties. He knew me, yet gave no greeting; was glad to see a woman's face, yet had no smile wherewith to welcome it; felt that he was dying, yet uttered no farewell. He was too far across the river to return or linger now; departing thought, strength, breath, were spent in one grateful look, one murmur of submission to the last pang he could ever feel. His lips moved, and, bending to them, a whisper chilled my cheek, as it shaped the broken words,—

"I'd 'a' done it,—but it's better so,—I'm satisfied."

Ah! well he might be,—for, as he turned his face from the shadow of the life that was, the sunshine of the life to be touched it with a beautiful content, and in the drawing of a breath my contraband found wife and home, eternal liberty and God.

APPENDIX

The United States Sanitary Commission

by Elisha Harris

$\mathcal{I}$NCIDENTAL to its great
work of ministering to the sick and wounded of the Western armies and
navy, and of promoting the health and energy of our soldiers in the field,
the Western Sanitary Commission has felt itself called to devote a portion
of its labors to the relief of forty thousand freedmen, along the banks of
the Mississippi river, from Columbus, Ky., to Natchez, many of whom, in
their transition from the ownership and control of slave masters, to the
condition of freedmen, have suffered untold hardships and privations, in

Reprinted from the *North American Review* 203 (April 1864).

a country stripped by the ravages of war, with no demand for labor, except in a few favored localities, nor any means of providing for their most urgent wants, food, clothing, and shelter. Seeing in them the victims of a life-long oppression, thrown destitute and almost naked upon the tender mercies of our armies in the field, many of them dying of exposure, hardship, and disease, the members of the Western Commission could not turn a deaf ear to their silent appeals for assistance and Christian sympathy.

Their attention was first called to the sufferings of these people at Helena, in the beginning of the winter of 1862–3, where there were between three and four thousand, men, women and children, part of them living in a place back of the town, established for them, by Gen. C. C. Washburne, the previous summer, called "Camp Ethiopia," in the condemned and cast-off tents of the army, and in caves and shelters of brush—the best arrangement that could be made at the time, but wholly insufficient for winter. Others dwelt in the poorer houses of the town, sixteen and twenty persons occupying the same room, and others still in the few huts that remained on the neighboring plantations. The able-bodied men had been worked very hard on the fortifications of the place, and by the quartermasters, in unloading coal from barges and freight from steamboats, and also as grave-diggers, teamsters and wood choppers, and in all manner of fatigue duty. For these services many of them never received any compensation, through the neglect of the officers, having them in charge, to keep proper pay rolls, and the indifference of several of the military commanders, immediately succeeding Maj. Gen. Curtis. At one time an order was issued forbidding their payment, on the ground that their masters would have a claim against the Government for their services. All the while they were compelled to do most of the hard work of the place, and press-gangs were sent out to take them in the streets and put them to work, sometimes by night as well as by day, taking no account of their names or labor, and dismissing them without compensation. Sometimes they were shot down, and murdered with impunity.

Under such circumstances they were not able to provide for their families, and rations had to be drawn for them from the Government. Herded together as they were, in camps and the poorest dwellings, it was no wonder that they sickened and died at a fearful rate. The writer of this, who was then on duty at Helena, has seen the streets patroled by mounted orderlies, to gather up the "contrabands," as they were called, for forced labor, while their women and children were driven from their little houses, to Camp Ethiopia, under an arbitrary military rule, with a view of expelling them from the town; and there being no additional shelter at the camp, they had to suffer there, till the order became partially a dead letter, by reason of its inhumanity. A military order was at one time issued, to carry them beyond the lines, under which many of them were delivered up to rebel masters, in violation of the Articles of War. With hundreds of sick, their only hospital was a small building, not sufficient for the care of twenty persons.

It was under these circumstances, that the Western Sanitary Commission, early in January, 1863, sent to Helena, that excellent and philanthropic woman, Miss Maria R. Mann, with a large supply of sanitary stores, clothing, hospital goods, furniture, stove, &c., to fit up a better hospital for the sick of this class, and to minister generally to their wants.

At this time, Rev. Samuel Sawyer, chaplain of the 47th Indiana infantry, and Rev. J. G. Forman, chaplain of the 3d Missouri infantry, both of them on detached service at Helena, were doing what they could for these poor people, and welcomed to the arrival of Miss Mann with great satisfaction. Mr. F. secured rooms for her and her stores in the same house occupied by himself and others, and the work of amelioration was immediately commenced. The hospital was soon renovated: and a month or two later, on the removal of a portion of the army, a larger and better building was obtained, when the sick of the freed people were better situated, and army surgeons were detailed to attend them. It was now known that a change of policy towards the emancipated people had been inaugurated by the Government. Adjutant General Thomas was on his way to look after these people, and organize regiments of fighting men from them, and the military commanders became more willing to grant favors in their behalf.

In the Spring a splendid regiment of the 1st Arkansas infantry, A. D., was recruited in a few days, commanded by Col. Wm. F. Wood, and a second was commenced. Miss Mann remained till the following August, performing a great amount of useful service to the wives and children of these men, giving clothing to the poor and needy, selling to those who had money to buy with, and replenishing her stock with the proceeds; teaching women to cut and make their own garments, providing medicines for the sick, visiting them in their camps and dwellings, giving them excellent advice, and in every possible way improving their condition.

Her labors there were also sustained by friends in New England, with whom she was in correspondence, and several thousand dollars worth of clothing, material for clothing, medicines, etc., were used by her in the most judicious manner, Rev. Dr. Eliot, at St. Louis, acting for the Commission, as Treasurer of a special fund for this purpose, contributed mostly by humane people in New England. Rev. Jonathan E. Thomas, chaplain 56th Ohio infantry, was also detailed to assist in this work, and his humanity and kindness to the poor "contrabands," as well as the faithful service of Rev. Mr. Sawyer, and the devoted labors of Miss Mann, will long be remembered by them, and by the writer of this sketch, who was providentially associated with them, for a time, in their benevolent work. It is due to Major Generals S. R. Curtis, C. C. Washburne, and Prentiss, who were in command at Helena for a brief period, to say that it was not during their administration of affairs that the evils were narrated occurred, and that they were always ready to do whatever was in their power, for the amelioration of the condition of the colored people at that post.

During the month of October, '63, the condition of the freed people, along the Mississippi river, again enlisted the earnest consideration of the Western Sanitary Commission. The same state of things that had existed at Helena, was reported as existing at many other points, between Columbus, Kentucky, and Natchez, chiefly the result of neglect, inability to procure remunerative employment, failure of quartermasters to enroll and pay the freedmen their wages, and the helpless condition of many, in consequence of the taking of the strong and able-bodied men for United States soldiers, leaving their wives and children, for a time, unprovided for.

On the 6th of November the Commission addressed a letter to the President of the United States, calling his attention to the condition of these people, the necessity of assistance, before another winter should set in, and proposing to assume the labor of soliciting contributions and extending relief, as an incidental part of its work. The proposal was favorably regarded, assurances were given by the Secretary of War that all possible aid would be rendered, in the way of transportation and otherwise, and, a few weeks later, Mr. Yeatman made a special visit down the river, to ascertain and report the actual state of things.

At the same time, Maj. Gen. Schofield, who gave his hearty approval and sympathy to the work, detailed, by special order, Chaplain H. D. Fisher, of the 5th Kansas Cavalry, to visit New England, under the direction of the Commission, and make a suitable appeal for contributions for this object. Mr. Fisher's visit was entirely successful, and very large contributions of clothing, material for clothing, shoes, and other necessary articles, amounting in value to about $30,000, and $13,000 in money, were obtained, by a committee in Boston, composed of Chas. G. Loring, *Chairman,* M. S. Scudder, *Secretary,* Alpheus Hardy, *Treasurer,* A. A. Lawrence, James M. Barnard, Wm. Endicott, Jr., Edward Atkinson, and sixteen others. These contributions came from Boston, Salem and other neighboring towns and cities, to whom the appeals of the Western Sanitary Commission have never been made in vain. Many valuable boxes of clothing material and shoes were sent by the Boston Educational Commission for Freedmen, of which Messrs. Barnard, Atkinson and Endicott, of the other committee, were also members.

On the 17th of December, Mr. Yeatman returned from his first visit to the freedmen of the lower Mississippi, and made a full report to the Commission, of which five thousand copies were printed and circulated. He stopped at Island No. 10, at Memphis, Helena, Goodrich's Landing, Milliken's Bend, Young's Point and Vicksburg, the plantations of Jeff and Joe Davis, and at Natchez, and returning, visited some of these points a second time.

The report, consisting of sixteen pages of closely printed matter, is so full of information that it is impossible to make even an abstract of it for this work. It is sufficient to say, that he found about forty thousand of these people in camps, at the above and other places, between Cairo and Natchez, in various degrees of poverty and wretchedness; that among them he found several volunteer agents, missionaries, and teachers, from the United Presbyterians, the Friends, and the Freedmen's Aid Associations, laboring for their benefit as well as they could, without system or co-operation; that in the cotton growing region, from Goodrich's Landing to Vicksburg, on the abandoned plantations, leased by the Government, he saw over twenty colored men, and heard of others who had raised from five to ten bales of cotton, on their own account, proving their capacity for self-maintenance, with a fair chance; that where they were laboring under the lessees their wages were wholly inadequate, being but five dollars per month for women, and seven dollars per month for men, with subsistence of the poorest kind; that they suffered many wrongs under this system; that when they were employed by Government Quartermasters, to cut wood for steamboats, they were frequently not paid; that they were charged an unreasonable price for goods, and were really suffering wrongs and hardships, equal to those they had borne in a state of slavery, while they were enjoying none of the blessings of liberty.

Mr. Yeatman, in his report, thus sets forth some of the wrongs of these people: "Within the city of Memphis, not directly connected with any of the camps, or with the colored regiments, there are some *three thousand* freed men and women, mostly freed men, who are employed in various ways, and at various rates of compensation. Those employed by Government, receive but ten dollars per month, while many could readily earn from thirty to fifty dollars per month. Those thus employed are outside of the military organization.

"To give an instance: One quartermaster told me that he had in his employment, a harness maker, to whom he could only pay ten dollars per month, while he was paying white men, doing the same work, forty-five dollars per month; and that the colored man could readily procure the same wages, were he allowed to seek a market for his labor in the same town. I saw a number of colored men pressed into service, (not military,) to labor at the rate of ten dollars per month, one of whom petitioned to be released, as he had a good situation at thirty dollars per month. The firemen on the steamboat on which I was a passenger from St. Louis to Memphis, were all colored, and were receiving forty-five dollars per month. These men were afraid to go ashore at Memphis, for fear of being picked up and forced into Government employment, at less than one-fourth their existing wages.

"Besides the fact that men are thus pressed into service, thousands have been employed for weeks and months, who have never received anything but promises to pay. This negligence and failure to comply with obligations, have greatly disheartened the poor slave, who comes forth at the call of the President, and supposes himself a free man, and that, by leaving his rebel master, he is inflicting a blow on the enemy, ceasing to labor and to provide food for him and for the armies of the rebellion. Thus he was promised freedom, but how is it with him? He is seized in the street, and ordered to go and help unload a steamboat, for which he will be paid, or sent to work in the trenches, or to labor for some quartermaster, or to chop wood for the Government. He labors for months, and at last is only paid with promises, unless perchance it may be with kicks, cuffs, and curses.

"Under such treatment, he feels that he has exchanged one master for many masters; these continued abuses sadden and depress him, and he sighs to return to his former home and master. He, at least, fed, clothed, and sheltered him. Something should be done, and I doubt not, will be done, to correct these terrible abuses, when the proper authorities are made to comprehend them. The President's proclamation should not thus be made a living lie, as the Declaration of Independence has too long been, in asserting the inalienable rights of man, while the nation continued to hold millions of human beings in bondage."

In another place he says:

"The poor negroes are everywhere greatly depressed at their condition. They all testify that if they were only paid their little wages as they earn them, so that they could purchase clothing, and were furnished with the provisions promised, they could stand it; but to work and get poorly paid, poorly fed, and not doctored when sick, is more than they can endure. Among the thousands whom I questioned, none showed the least unwillingness to work. If they could only be paid fair wages, they would be contented and happy. They do not realize that they are free men. They say that they are told they are, but then they are taken and hired out to men who treat them, so far as providing for them is concerned, far worse than their secesh masters did. Besides this they feel that their pay or hire is lower now than it was when the secesh used to hire them. This is true."

And yet, under all their accumulated wrongs, these people manifest a wonderful faith in Divine Providence; they seem to be sensible that God has some better thing in store for them, and to realize that, through this wilderness of suffering and sorrow is the only path to their deliverance. Mrs. Porter, at Camp Holly Spring, near Memphis, related to Mr. Yeatman an instance of this. When she first went there to teach, an old negro came out to meet her, whose head had been whitened by the frosts of ninety winters, and who was almost blind, supporting himself by his staff. With his hand stretched forth he accosted her, saying, "Well, you hab come at las'. I'se been 'spectin' you, lookin' for you, for de las' twenty years. I knowed you would come, and now I rejoice." She said, "I have come to teach you." "Yes, yes, I know it, and I tank de Lord."

At this same camp Mr. Yeatman saw a colored man, who, after his return from his work, was seated in his cabin, surrounded by his own children and a few others from the adjoining cabins, teaching them their lessons for the morrow. At another school he met an old woman, aged eighty-five, who was intent on her books. When asked if she was not too old to begin to learn, she said, "No," that she must learn now or not at all, as she had but little time left, and she must make the most of it. When asked what good it would do her, she said "she could read de bible, and teach de young." At other places similar instances of faith and piety, and the desire of knowledge, were witnessed.

Mr. Yeatman was most favorably impressed with the capacity of the negroes to become soldiers. He gives an account of several successful expeditions, under Col. Farrar, at Natchez, in which they brought in prisoners. In one instance he says, "The prisoners were much chagrined at being taken by negroes, and asked if they could not have another guard to take them through town; but as they were captured by negroes, they had to be guarded and escorted by them."

He says of another experience he had, "In going from Goodrich's Landing to Milliken's Bend, I was escorted by twenty colored troops, mounted on mules captured from the enemy. They rode gallantly and fearlessly, putting out their advance guard and arranging themselves in true military order, conducting themselves with as much propriety as an equal number of well behaved gentlemen. When we arrived at the Bend, and dashed into the fort, surrounded by troops, my companion—Dr. May—and myself, dressed in citizen's clothes, and mounted in an old wagon, were taken for prisoners, and our escort was called out to by the soldiers, "Rebs! Rebs!" and an amount of ivory displayed that I have seldom seen exceeded.

"I could but compare my first visit to this point years ago, when I landed to take charge of a large estate, as executor, with my present one. It was here in these swamps that I first saw and knew what a dead, leaden thing slavery is, and the wrong and injustice which could be inflicted, even by one, considered the kindest and most humane of masters. I doubt not the seed was then sown in my heart which has since germinated, and makes me now not only willing, but anxious to labor for these poor sons of soil. What a revolution a few short years has brought about! Who can doubt that an infinitely wise and just God governs the world?"

On submitting his report to the Commission, Mr. Yeatman was delegated to visit Washington, and present this subject to the Government. In doing so, he also presented a series of printed "suggestions of a plan of organization for freed labor and the leasing of plantations along the Mississippi river." His report and suggestions were most favorably received at Washington, and he was urged and authorized to accompany Mr. W. P. Mellen, the special supervising agent of the Treasury Department, to Vicksburg, to mature and carry them into effect. This trust of the Government he accepted, as a voluntary work, declining an official position, which was offered him; and he proceeded a second time, now in company with Mr. Mellen, to the region of the leased plantations; near Vicksburg.

The new plan of labor—in view of the high price of cotton, and the profit to be derived from its cultivation—provided that the freedmen should receive from $12 to $25 a month, according to age, sex, ability, etc.; that there should be a secure method of enforcing the contract for labor and wages; that the lessee should furnish goods at an advance of ten per cent. on the cost; that there should be established "Home Farms," under a superintendent, for the young and old, the infirm and destitute; that there should be schools and teachers, for all children under twelve years old; and that a tax should be paid to the Government of four dollars, on each bale of cotton raised, and of two cents per pound, for the support of the "Home Farms," and the schools; and that the system should be carried out by commissioners of plantations, acting under the Treasury Department, who should see that justice is administered; that the freed people are treated as free, and encouraged to respect and observe the institutions of religion, marriage, and all the customs of virtuous and civilized society, and to become worthy of the blessings of a Christian civilization.

On their way down the river, Messrs. Mellen and Yeatman had a new form of lease, and printed regulations prepared at Memphis, and on arriving at Vicksburg, inaugurated the new order of things. At first it met with some opposition from the old lessees, who saw in it a diminution of their gains; but seeing that it was promulgated with authority, it was acquiesced in, local agents were appointed, and about six hundred plantations were immediately leased, under the new system.

The withdrawal of the troops, from some of the districts, had caused considerable discouragement at first, but on a second visit of Messrs. Mellen and Yeatman to Washington, the Secretary of War was induced to give the services of the Marine Brigade, for the purpose of affording protection to the plantations and freed people; and the work of growing cotton, the present year, is already progressing with satisfaction to all concerned, with a great improvement in the prospects of the laborers, and their ultimate success as independent cultivators of the soil; for the more intelligent of them do not fail to see the advantages of possessing land of their own, and are ambitious to work for themselves, instead of a master. In almost every instance where they attempted, last year, to cultivate cotton, on their own account, they were entirely successful, numerous instances of which Mr. Yeatman gave in his published report.

While these changes were being effected, a National Freedmen's Relief Association had been organized in New York city, and a Northwestern Freedmen's Relief Commission at Chicago, besides which there were two similar associations already existing at Cincinnati, and another was formed at Indianapolis. Harmonious relations were at once established between these Associations and the Western Sanitary Commission.

On the 11th December, Messrs. Wm. L. Marsh and H. R. Foster, from the National Freedmen's Relief Association of New York, arrived at St. Louis, with a letter of introduction from Hon. F. G. Shaw, the President of the Association, on their way to Vicksburg, to establish an agency there, for the distribution of goods to the needy; the sale of them to those who could pay, and for the employment of teachers to instruct the people. Mr. Yeatman was at the time down the river; but these gentlemen, seeing the advantages of co-operation and unity of purpose, consented to act also as agents of the Western Sanitary Commission, and thereby secured an arrangement for the re-shipment of their goods from St. Louis to Vicksburg, which they were expecting from New York, and the Commission also secured the benefit of their valuable services, as agents in the field.

Very large shipments of clothing soon began to arrive from New York, directed to Mr. Marsh, and were forwarded with shipments from the Western Sanitary Commission, at the earliest period. They were unfortunately delayed several weeks by the severe cold of December and January, which closed the navigation for awhile, but were ultimately received, and accomplished great good. Of the proceeds of the goods sold by these gentlemen, on account of the Western Sanitary Commission, they have returned $1000. Their services have been in every respect most useful and satisfactory, and have been extended to Natchez, and other places besides Vicksburg.

During the winter they wrote to the Commission to send them two teachers, to assist in the work of instruction and distribution at Vicksburg. Miss A. M. Knight, of Sun Prairie, Wis., and Miss Sarah J. Hagar, of this city, were commissioned, and their services have been very acceptable and useful. In February, Mrs. Lydia H. Daggett, of Boston, a very excellent and capable person, was sent into the same field, to act under the direction of Mr. Marsh.

Within a few days, the friends of Miss Hagar have been pained to receive the news of her unexpected death, at Vicksburg, from a sudden attack of disease. She was a devoted, and estimable young woman. It is due to her memory, that the following letter, from Mr. Marsh, should have a place here, since she died in the service of the Commission, and in so good a cause.

"NATCHEZ, *May* 6, 1864.

"REV. J. G. FORMAN,

"*Sec'ry Western Sanitary Commission:*

"MY DEAR SIR—You have already received from Mr. Mann, the sad intelligence of the death of Miss Hagar, one of the teachers sent by you, to labor among the freed people in this valley.

"I was at Natchez when she was taken ill, and did not receive intelligence of it in time to reach Vicksburg, until after her death, which occurred on Tuesday, May 3d.

"In her death, the Association have lost a most *earnest*, devoted and Christian laborer. She entered upon her duties at a time of great suffering and destitution, among the freedmen, at Vicksburg, and when we were much in need of aid. The fidelity with which she performed her labors, and the deep interest she manifested in them, soon endeared her to us all. We shall miss her sorely; but the noble example she has left us, will encourage us to greater efforts and more patient toil. She seemed to realize the magnitude and importance of the work upon which she had entered, and the need of Divine assistance, in its performance. She seemed also to realize what sacrifice *might be* demanded of one engaged in a work like this, and the summons, although sudden, did not find her unprepared to meet it. She has done a noble work, and *done it well*. The sacrifice she made, is the greatest one that can be made for any cause, the *sacrifice of life*. 'Greater love than this, hath no man; that a man lay down his life for his friends.' She has gone to receive her reward.

"The family thus suddenly bereaved, and plunged in affliction, by this sad occurrence, has our sympathies and prayers. When they meet to perform the last sad rites due to the dead, may they not look in the close, narrow, burial-case for their loved one, but rather raise their eyes to behold a spirit, freed from earthly fetters, clothed in spotless robes, and wearing the crown bestowed only upon those who prove faithful to the end.   Respectfully,

"W. L. MARSH."

Besides the labors of Messrs. Marsh and Foster at Vicksburg, the regular agent of the Commission, Mr. N. M. Mann, has taken a deep interest in the same work, and though much occupied in the superintendence of the Soldiers' Home, and the care of the refugees, he has found time to lend a helping hand. An interesting letter was received from him, dated the 7th of March, in which he gives a full account of the arrival of the four thousand five hundred freedmen, who returned with Gen'l Sherman's Army, from Meridian, and of his distribution of food and clothing among them. "Anticipating a need," he says, "I had drawn heavily on the Commissary for bread and had a large amount on hand. I had the ambulance of the Western Sanitary Commission loaded with this bread, and taking along half a dozen kind-hearted soldiers, we went the whole length of this wagon train and gave to each family a loaf or two. It was but a little thing to do, but the eagerness with which they took and ate it told how grateful it was to them. I assure you I never was more happy than that night, amid all that wretchedness, giving bread to those hungry creatures. That night they lay on the levee, in their wagons, and on the ground. Many who came from plantations this side of Jackson were without conveyances, having walked in, bearing their 'effects' on their heads. The next morning they were sent on Steamboats to camps at Davis' Bend, and Oswego Landing, and in company with Mrs. Harvey, of Wisconsin, and Miss Dart, a teacher from New England, I went to Oswego with a quantity of old clothing, furnished by the National Freedmen's Relief Association, of New York, for distribution. To all the most destitute, or rather the most torn and naked, for all are destitute, we gave some of the more necessary articles of clothing. I only wish that the donors of those articles could have witnessed the distribution. I do not know where on the face of the globe, out of the Southern Confederacy, a thousand people could be got together that would present to charity so strong an appeal as these. I wish I could send to every Northern home of plenty, a photograph of these barefooted, ragged, half-naked creatures, as they appeared to me that day. They had been fed, and although their destitute, filthy, tattered and homeless condition was enough to draw tears from a heart of stone, many were cheerful and gave evidence that, with a very little comfort, they would be happy. The endurance of the negro has always been a marvel. It was never so much so as now. It is his difference from the white man, in this respect, that is to save him, if he is saved, in this great trial.''

The Union refugees have also received a share in the labors of the Western Sanitary Commission. During the fall and winter of 1861–2 many refugees were driven, by the rebels, from the interior and southwest parts of Missouri to St. Louis, and were in a condition of want and suffering. A home, on Elm street, was opened for the most helpless and destitute, and others were assisted, according to their necessities. Mr. John Cavender, an old and respectable citizen, eminent for his integrity and christian character, devoted his whole time to their care. A fund was raised at first, by a call of the Western Sanitary Commission, amounting to about $3,800, besides a large amount of clothing. A further sum of $15,000 was raised by an order of Maj. Gen. Halleck, by assessing the wealthy class of secessionists, in St. Louis, for this object, and from this resource Mr. Cavender was able to render very important aid to these persecuted and destitute people. For two years he took almost the entire charge of this work, in which he had the counsel of the members of the Commission, and was sometimes aided with funds for the purpose, when other sources failed. During the winter of 1863, Mr. Cavender, whose health had been failing, was taken sick and died, and there was but little demand from that time, till the next September, for any further aid to the refugees. In this charitable service no one could have been more faithful and constant than Mr. Cavender had been; and in other relations and duties, during an honorable and well spent life, he had been distinguished as the upright citizen, and patron of christian learning and philanthropy, and his death was greatly lamented.

In August, '63, there began to be further arrivals of destitute refugees from Arkansas, Tennessee, Mississippi, Alabama, Louisiana, and Texas. Many of them were women, with small children, poorly clad, often bare-footed, brought up the river on Government steamers, and landed here, without the means of procuring a place of shelter for a single night. Their husbands had been killed in the war, had been murdered by guerrillas, had been conscripted into the rebel army, or had died from the effects of exposure in lying out in the woods, in dens and caves of the earth, to escape the blood-hounds of the rebel conscription. At first these poor refugee families fell into the hands of the police but the police station was not a fit place for them, although some of them found shelter there.

One day, late in August, the President of the Commission was called to see what could be done for a poor blind woman, and her family of six children, who had walked all the way from Arkansas to Rolla, Mo., her little children leading her several hundred miles by the hand, and from Rolla they had been brought on the cars to St. Louis, as a charity. They were in an upper unfurnished room of the Pacific hotel, the woman, and a boy about twelve years old, being sick, and she totally blind. They sat upon the floor, clothed in rags, and presented a sight that would have moved the stoutest heart to pity and to tears.

The children of this woman, whose name was Mrs. Hargrave, were adopted by Rev. Dr. Eliot, and placed in the Mission school on Eighth street, and the mother was sent to the St. Louis hospital, kept by the Sisters of Charity. Her youngest children she had never seen, they having been born since she became blind. The parting of the blind mother from her little ones was a touching scene. But she gave them up willingly, knowing it to be a necessity, and for their good. At the Sisters' hospital, her health, after several months, was restored, and, by a surgical operation of Dr. Pope, the cataracts were removed from her eyes, and she was able to see. Her children were then brought to her, and the meeting can be better imagined than described.

A little later, another refugee mother came, and, with two little children, stood at the door of the Commission, on Fifth street, having no place to go. They were barefooted, dusty with travel, and miserably clad. The mother told her sad story.

Her husband had been murdered by guerrillas, near Fort Smith, Ark., and she had walked, with her children, to Rolla, riding part of the way in

Government wagons, and had reached St. Louis, as a place of refuge. She had to stay at the police station that night. The next day, three women and children arrived from Jackson, Tenn., in an equally destitute condition. There was no alternative but to open another refuge home. The President of the Commission rented the house, 39 Walnut street, for the purpose, on the 1st of September, and from that date to the present, not less than fifteen hundred refugees have been sheltered, provided for, or sent on their way to friends, or places of employment, in the free States. By an arrangement with Generals Schofield and Rosecrans, rations and fuel are allowed from the Government, and the rent is paid by the Quartermaster; but the incidental expenses of the home, and the charities in clothing, money, &c., are provided by the Commission. It is under the superintendence of Rev. Mr. Forman, the Secretary of the Commission, and its domestic arrangements are conducted by Miss M. Elliott, as Matron, who, in a spirit of true self-sacrifice, devotes her time and strength to the service of these poor outcasts from the rebellion. The expenses and charities of the Home, and for destitute refugee families in the city, and to those going beyond St. Louis, have been about $1,000 in six months, beyond the aid received from the Government in rations, fuel, rent, and transportation. Several valuable boxes of clothing have been received from New England; also contributions of money from Boston, from the Ladies' Loyal League, of St. Louis, and from various other sources. The receipts for this charity and for the Freedmen, and the disbursements are kept separate from the other funds and resources of the Commission, so that there is no misappropriation of what is designed for the soldiers to these objects. Contributors are always requested to designate the object of their charities, and if no designation is made, they go into the sanitary fund.

The number of refugees at Pilot Knob, at the present time, is over 1700 persons, mostly women and children. They are chiefly from Arkansas, and are under the superintendence of a faithful and excellent man, Chaplain A. Wright, who has been specially assigned to that duty. Contributions to the value of several thousand dollars in goods, clothing, shoes, medicines for the sick, hardware and sash to assist in building cheap houses, and over $1000 in money have been sent to Mr. Wright, and expended in a judicious manner. At a time of special distress the Commission sent him fifteen barrels of clothing, eighty dollars in material for clothing, (purchased by Mrs. General Fisk) twenty dollars in money, sixty dollars in medicines, thirty dollars worth of glazed sash, half a dozen axes for women, who cut their own wood; and of the other contributions a large portion was collected by Mrs. Fisk, who made visits to Pilot Knob, and was most energetic and successful in her endeavors to relieve and benefit these poor people. Brig. Gen. Fisk, also, while commanding the District, did every thing in his power to minister to their wants.

The Western Commission also responded to an appeal from Mr. J. R. Brown, agent U.S. Sanitary Commission at Leavenworth City, for aid to refugees at that post, and at Fort Scott, Kansas, and sent thirty boxes of clothing to those points, and a thousand Union Spellers for schools of the freed children at Leavenworth.

At Rolla, Springfield, Cape Girardeau, Cairo, Columbus, Memphis, Helena, and Vicksburg, there are multitudes of these poor refugees, numbered by thousands, who have come to us from rebel persecution and outrage, or have been driven, by the ravages of war, and the destitution of food and clothing, to seek a refuge within our lines. Humanity requires that they should be aided, at least to the extent of saving life, and to enable them to reach places, where employment and subsistance can be found.

Recently a necessity has arisen for a Refugee Home at Vicksburg, and the Commission has established one there, under the superintendence of Mr. Mann, with Mrs. Maria Brooks for matron. It was opened on the 1st of April, and has already received and aided 2,160 of these poor people. On the 7th of May, there were 620 remaining, mostly women and children. Transportation had been furnished to those wishing to emigrate North, and employment for the able-bodied men.

The large number of destitute white children, belonging to these families, having no means of instruction, has induced the Commission to send a teacher, Miss G. C. Chapman, to Vicksburg, to open a school for them, in connection with the Home, also under Mr. Mann's superintendence. This lady is now on her way, with a supply of school books for this purpose.

In all these enterprises of benevolence, Mr. Mann, as the agent of the Commission, has had the sanction, advice and co-operation of General McArthur, commanding at Vicksburg, who has assigned to the Commission suitable buildings for the purpose, and shown his great friendliness in this and many other ways.